○○○○○○○○○○○○○○○○○●○○○○○○○○○○○○○○○○○○○○○○●○○○

Diggers of Lost Treasure

Kathleen Fidler

○○○

DIGGERS OF LOST TREASURE

London EPWORTH PRESS

To the Memory of my Father
FRANCIS FIDLER
who encouraged my love of
Archaeology

First published by
Epworth Press 1972

Printed in Great Britain by
Morrison & Gibb Ltd,
London and Edinburgh

SBN 7162 0213 1

Inquiries should be sent to
The Methodist Publishing House
The Book Room
2 Chester House
Pages Lane
London N10 1PZ

Contents

ACKNOWLEDGEMENT

The publisher's thanks are due to
Radio Times Hulton Picture Library
for permission to reproduce the illustrations
that appear on pages 10, 15, 19, 27, 31, 33, 61,
63, 79, 85, 92, 94, 99, 105, 109, 113,
114, 117, 121, 131, 133, 137, 145, 151, 152, 153

FOREWORD

○○○

Though Austen Henry Layard was British and Henry Schliemann was German, their lives had a great deal in common. They lived at the same time during the reign of Queen Victoria in the nineteenth century. They were the first searchers for ancient buried cities in the Near East and the first men to dig them out, Layard at Nineveh and Babylon; Schliemann at Mycenae and Troy.

For both of them the dream of finding buried cities began when they were children. Both were bookworms. Henry Layard had his imagination stirred by *Tales of the Arabian Nights*; Henry Schliemann received a book about Troy for a Christmas present. Each vowed secretly to himself that some day he would go in search of these lost cities and find buried treasure.

Neither of them enjoyed an entirely happy childhood. Layard was buffeted from school to school abroad and in Britain. Schliemann's father became a drunken wretch who could not pay for his son's schooling. Just as the boy was progressing well he had to leave school at an early age to earn his own living.

Both boys were penniless youths and had to take what

work was offered to them; Layard as a junior clerk in his
uncle's law office; Schliemann as a grocer's boy. When they
could stand the misery and dreariness of their occupations no
longer they each set out to seek his fortune in the world.
Layard set out for Ceylon, but fortune kept him in Asia
Minor; Schliemann tried to go to America, but shipwreck
brought him back to Europe. Chance played a part in shaping
the lives of both young men. They could both speak several
languages and quickly learned new ones, so their thoughts
turned naturally to travelling in distant lands. They had this
'gift of tongues' in common.

In later life each man married a beautiful wife much
younger than himself and enjoyed a very happy married life.
Indeed, Schliemann's wife was a partner with him in his
actual digging.

The two men made their childhood dreams come true, for
they found their lost cities and in them vast treasure that was
to enrich the museums of the world. Not only that, they
paved the way for other archaeologists to follow them, so
that the work they began was continued in Greece, Crete,
Asia Minor and Mesopotamia, and still goes on today.

PART ONE

○○

AUSTEN HENRY LAYARD

Austen Henry Layard
1817–94

CHAPTER ONE

○○○

Far to Go

There is an old idea that the circumstances of a child's birth will influence that child's life later on. Henry Austen Layard, as he was first named, was born in a Paris hotel in 1817 while his father and mother were travelling on the continent. Certainly Henry's whole life was full of journeys afterwards and he had indeed 'far to go'. He clearly remembered travelling to Italy when he was only three years old.

'I well remember crossing the Simplon Pass and travelling through Italy to Florence; the places where we stopped and slept; the abundance of fruit and the piles of grapes and figs at roadside stalls', he wrote later.

Henry's father, Henry Peter Layard, suffered greatly from a lung complaint, asthma. He had been a British official in Ceylon, but ill health had forced him to retire while he was still young. Henry's mother was the daughter of Nathaniel Austen, a banker in Ramsgate. She was pretty, with beautiful blue eyes, a sweet voice and a gentle manner, kind and generous. Henry loved his mother dearly.

'She was a great reader and delighted in history, biography and travels. She was a good and constant letter writer', Henry wrote of his mother many years later. Perhaps it was from his mother that he took his love of travel and history.

His father sought a place to live where he would be free from his asthma attacks. He found it in Florence in Italy. There Henry attended a nursery school kept by an English lady. Every day he was taken to school by Pachot, an old Frenchman who had been taken prisoner at the battle of Waterloo. Pachot became a manservant to the Layards and stayed with them all his life. Alongside the old man and the small boy there trotted 'Mouche', a black poodle, who carried a lighted lantern in his mouth when it was dark. Henry grew up speaking three languages—English, French and Italian.

The happy childhood in Florence was not to last. Mrs Layard had an elder brother, Benjamin Austen, who had very strong opinions and liked to tell other people what they ought to do.

'Italy is no place in which to bring up young Englishmen', he declared in a letter. 'They would be far better educated at home in England.'

Uncle Benjamin was a well-to-do lawyer with a good business, and Mrs Layard always regarded his word as law, so back to Ramsgate the Layard family went. Henry was placed at a preparatory school in Putney, but all that he could say of it later was that he 'learned but little there'.

Uncle Benjamin's advice was well meant but not very far-seeing. Mr Layard could not stand up to the sea winds and winter fogs at Ramsgate. His asthma became worse. It was plain he must seek a milder climate than Britain's, so this time the family went to Moulins in the very centre of France. Henry was left at school in Putney till the family were settled in the new home, then his father sent for him.

Though Henry was only eight years old, he was thrilled at the idea of making the long journey alone; and a long journey it was, for in those days there were no trains nor cars. Henry went by stage-coach, steamer across to France, then stage-coach again, with a stay in Paris while he changed coaches. The little lad was quite undaunted. A relative put him aboard a steamship for Calais. There he saw himself on the coach bound for Paris, where an acquaintance met him and took him to an hotel in Paris to wait till the coach departed for Moulins.

Henry enjoyed his couple of days in Paris exploring the city with his hotel landlady's daughter, a girl about his own age. Henry felt himself quite a seasoned traveller and, as his father might have done, he ordered a bottle of champagne with his dinner, which Mr Layard, to his amazement, found charged in the bill. History is silent as to whether Henry drank it all.

The journey to Moulins was a long and tiring one, but Henry enjoyed it. He wrote: 'I arrived late in the night at Moulins. I can remember vividly the scene in the yard at the inn where the coach stopped; the high-booted postillions dismounting, the passengers getting down, the stable-boys running about with lanterns and the steaming horses moving off to the stables. In the crowd I recognized my father who was waiting for me.'

This was the first of many long journeys that Henry Layard was to take alone.

At Moulins Henry was sent to a school where he was the only English boy. It was not more than ten years after the French defeat at Waterloo and the downfall of Napoleon, so there was still ill-feeling among the French for the English. Small Henry was the victim of it. He had many tough fights with his class-mates who tried to rub his nose upon the floor. Henry fought back. All the boys hated a very brutal teacher. They decided to get even with him and asked Henry how they should go about it. Henry suggested they should all unite in throwing things at the bullying teacher next time he took their class. The other boys seemed to welcome this suggestion. Henry was to lead off the attack: he was to be the first to throw an inkwell at the teacher! Henry's leading shot missed the man but hit the blackboard a resounding thump. To Henry's surprise no other inkwell followed suit. There was a dead silence. Henry looked round and saw every other boy with his head bent over his book. It had been a trap laid by his class-mates to catch him out and bring punishment upon his head. The master stalked towards him, wielding a heavy ruler, and Henry got a severe beating. After that he was locked in a cellar for twenty-four hours and only given a thin vegetable soup. Henry stuck it out bravely at school, whacked by the masters and attacked by the boys. Then one day he came home with his cheek cut open by a blow from a school-mate. Mrs Layard was horrified and his parents decided to remove him from this unhappy school.

It was found, too, that Moulins did not suit Mr Layard's health, so the whole family removed to Geneva to try the Swiss climate. Once again Henry's school was changed. This time, though he often got into trouble, he was far happier. His schoolmaster recognized his independent spirit. Layard himself said, 'He was much kinder to me than I deserved. I no doubt caused a lot of trouble and vexation to my masters.'

At this school, however, Henry learned to swim, and also the headmaster took his pupils on walking tours and climbing trips among the mountains. Henry revelled in these and grew hardy and daring.

If Geneva suited Henry it did not suit his father. Once again the Layards removed and returned to Florence, where Mr Layard's health had been much better. They hired a large carriage and with their four sons, two English maids, and Pachot the manservant, they made their way over the Simplon Pass into Italy. The boys had to get down from the carriage and walk up the hills to ease the horses, but Henry

Florence as it was in Layard's boyhood

and his brother Edgar found this great fun and started collecting butterflies.

In Florence Mr Layard rented an old house called the Rucellai Palace. The Rucellai family lived on the top floors and let the lower floors to the English family. A room on the lower floor was always kept locked. Henry's curiosity was excited by it.

'I think Bluebeard's wives are in there,' he confided to Pachot, always his friend. 'I mean to see what is inside.'

His chance came when his parents were away one day and Henry found a bunch of keys. He persuaded Pachot to try them in the forbidden lock. Perhaps Pachot was curious too. When the door opened they found themselves in a private chapel. They tiptoed across the chapel in the half-darkness, Pachot carrying a candle. The light fell on a glass-sided coffin in which was the embalmed body of a lady clothed in white. Henry let out a shriek of terror. She was no Bluebeard's wife, however, but had been a very saintly member

of the Rucellai family long ago. It was the custom of Italians
in the Middle Ages to preserve the bodies of their saints and
place them in glass coffins where they could be venerated.
Henry's curiosity was cured and afterwards he left the chapel
severely alone. 'I had nightmares about it for months afterwards, though,' he confessed.

Once again Henry went to a new school, this time a day-
school run by Signor Rellini, the 'Instituto'. There Henry
learned to speak very fluent Italian. At this school he had the
company of the children of Walter Savage Landor, an English
writer and poet. Truth to tell, this happy little band of
children often ran wild and played truant from school. Henry
was caught out by Signor Rellini, though, when the Signor
called at his home to enquire after his health, after two or
three days of Henry skipping school!

It was about this time that Mr Layard took a great interest
in Henry's reading and gave him the run of his library. Henry
read Shakespeare, Ben Jonson, and most of the finest literature, but his favourite of all was *The Arabian Nights' Entertainments*. This book contained a thousand and one stories
told by the Sultan's favourite wife to amuse the Sultan. They
were really fairy stories that held all the mystery of Arabia.
Henry's imagination was fired by it. 'I thought and dreamed
of little else but djinns and ghouls and fairies and lovely
princesses until I believed in their existence.'

Henry read, too, of Sinbad the Sailor and his father told him
stories of Ceylon. He made up his mind that when he grew
up he would travel in these mysterious eastern countries. It
was the book *The Arabian Nights* more than any other that
fired his youthful imagination and was to send him later on
the adventurous journey that took him to Nineveh.

Henry loved Florence. He went with his father to explore
the city, its churches and palaces and its art galleries. He loved
to show their English visitors around. He was tremendously

happy even though he was receiving rather a patchy education.

Into this happy life Uncle Benjamin Austen intruded once more like a spectre at the feast! He did not approve of this happy-go-lucky way of life. In a letter he pointed out: 'Your sons are growing up and neither the schooling nor the atmosphere of Italy are proper preparation for the life of an English gentleman. It will soon be time to think of suitable careers for the boys, especially Henry who is now twelve.' He promised to do something for the boy 'but he must first attend an English school'. Afterwards he would take Henry as an apprentice into his own law office.

Once again there was dismay and upheaval in the Layard household. Back they went to England. Henry was utterly miserable at leaving Florence. Once again he was sent to school, this time to a boarding school at Richmond-on-Thames kept by the Reverend James Bewsher.

Bewsher was a kind headmaster, but Henry Layard was not popular with his school-mates. They jeered at his fluency in speaking French and Italian. *Latin* was the thing for an English gentleman to learn! Though it was fourteen years after the battle of Waterloo in 1815, anything French was still held in suspicion by English schoolboys. The Duke of Wellington, still a popular hero, was Prime Minister in 1829 when Henry joined the school. The boys called Henry 'French Froggie'. At his French school he had been bullied for being English: now he was mocked for his fluency in French!

Henry was a good athlete, an excellent swimmer and rower, but he took little interest in cricket or football. He would far rather go for long walks or take out a boat on the Thames. This too cut him off from his school-fellows. Since he was not going to a university his teachers did not take much interest in his studies.

Henry's parents had returned to Florence, so during the summer holidays Henry had to stay at school. He was not miserable, for he could go fishing when he liked or spend the time exploring the neighbourhood and making sketches. He liked drawing. He could sit with his nose in a book all day. He borrowed books on travel from a shop-library to which he paid a subscription out of his meagre pocket-money. Especially did he delight in books about the Near East, tales of Turkey, Mesopotamia, Arabia and Persia. Though he was not aware of it, the choice of his reading was pointing the way he was later to go.

Christmas he spent with his Uncle Benjamin and Aunt Sara Austen in London. To his joy the British Museum was near to his uncle's house. He spent hours in the Museum looking at its collections. Once again he did not know at the time the big influence the British Museum was to have on his life. Uncle Benjamin did not approve of this 'time wasting'.

'You would be better to spend your time reading *Blackstone's Commentaries on the Laws of England* and prepare yourself for the study of the law', he told Henry.

Henry found *Blackstone's Commentaries* utterly dreary. He kept a book of travels or an historical novel hidden under the weighty Blackstone, that he could read when Uncle Austen disappeared and whip underneath when he heard him returning.

In 1833, when Henry Layard was sixteen, he left school and entered his uncle's law office as an apprentice clerk. He was never asked if he wanted to be a lawyer or not. It was all decided for him. In his secret heart Henry knew this was not what he really wanted.

He did not live with his uncle and aunt. A dreary back room was taken for him in a lodging house in New Ormond Street. His father allowed him eight pounds a month to pay for his lodging, food, books and clothes. He received no wage

from his uncle, for in those days law-apprentices had to *pay*
for their training. His uncle gave him his training free, that
and his dinner on Sunday. This was the 'something' he had
promised to do for his nephew.

Every day Henry worked from nine o'clock in the morning
at his uncle's office in Gray's Inn. He was kept copying legal
documents of land and property and people's wills till the
office work finished in the evening. It was monotonous,
weary work for a spirited lad. At the end of the day he had
a meal alone in a cheap eating-house in Fleet Street where a
chop cost him sixpence. His uncle expected him to return
to the office at night to study law books till his bed-time.
The office was cheerless and bitter cold in winter and his eyes
ached in the lamp-light. Often Henry fell asleep, in danger

The British Museum (Montagu House)
From an engraving of 1830

of falling from his perch on an office stool. It was a drab
miserable life and he hated the law books. He wrote: 'It soon
became evident to me that I should never master the science
of law or take any pleasure in it. Its study became, indeed,
repugnant to me and all my efforts to persevere in it were
vain.'

Instead of returning to Gray's Inn to study during the
evenings he went to his lodgings and played his flute, his
chief comfort. His good midday dinner on Sunday at the
Austens was something to which he looked forward all week,
not only because of the good food but because of the
company. His Aunt Sara often invited famous people to
dinner. There Henry met a well-known traveller, Sir Charles
Fellows, Joseph Turner, a great painter, and young Benjamin
Disraeli who was later Prime Minister. William Wordsworth,
the poet, was also a guest. They talked of Italy which they
both loved so much. Layard said of him: 'He inspired me
with the greatest respect and admiration. He was very kind
and allowed me to talk to him freely.'

Henry borrowed books from a friend who had a large
library.

'Soon every moment I could spare from my work at
Gray's Inn was devoted to general reading', he wrote. 'I
returned home as early as I was able from the office and passed
my evening with books. I have many a time gone without
my dinner in order to buy a coveted book.'

Meanwhile the Layard family had again returned to
England. Uncle Austen had told Mr Layard it was his duty
to come back and watch over his sons' education. Uncle
Austen was very good at pointing out their duty to other
people. This time his advice had a sad result. As the autumn
fogs descended Mr Layard was taken ill with lung trouble
and died very suddenly. It was a terrible shock to Henry,
for his father had been his great friend. Together, in Henry's

childhood, they had roamed Florence and his father had taught him a great deal about Italian art and history.

The next winter Henry himself fell ill. Possibly it was due to the shock of his father's death, but Henry blamed the work and confinement in a lawyer's office which he hated. His doctor advised that he should pass the summer holidays abroad. The first summer he went on a walking tour in Switzerland and northern Italy. He was overjoyed at being in Italy again. A note in his diary said, 'I was much interested in the Roman remains in the town of Aosta and spent a day exploring them'. His keen delight in the buildings left by former civilizations was already showing itself.

There followed other summer holidays abroad, France and Italy. In 1838 came a visit to Copenhagen. He records, 'I took at Copenhagen my first lesson in northern and prehistoric antiquities.' Yet again this was a pointer to the way his future was shaping.

The holidays were over all too soon: then came the dreaded return to the law office.

'The idea of following the profession of law became every day more hateful to me. I could not conceal my feelings on the subject from my uncle', he wrote.

Uncle Benjamin was disgusted at his nephew's failure to work hard at law studies. 'You cannot expect that I shall take you into the firm as a partner', he warned Henry.

Henry felt despairing. There seemed to be no future for him except as a poorly paid law-clerk, hating his job. Just when things seemed at their worst, help arrived from an unexpected quarter. Another uncle, Charles Layard, his father's brother, arrived from Ceylon.

Henry found that Uncle Charles had a sympathetic ear. He was sorry for the ambitious boy who was so eager to see the world.

'There is no hope of getting on in my Uncle Austen's

office,' he told Charles. 'I am very disappointed with my prospects.'

'Then why don't you come to Ceylon and work as a lawyer there?' Uncle Charles suggested. 'There are plenty of openings. You have only a few months to serve of your apprenticeship to your Uncle Austen. Next June you will be taking your examination at the Law Institution. Do you think you will pass?'

'I think I could if I put my mind to it,' Henry said candidly.

'Get that examination, then. It is all you will need in Ceylon.'

Henry set to work with a new heart, but Uncle Benjamin was very disapproving of the idea of going to Ceylon.

'It is my duty to warn you of the risks you are taking,' he told Henry. 'You might find yourself stranded in a strange country without any means of support.'

Henry was never one to be frightened by possible risks. His Uncle Benjamin should have known him better than that.

'*You* have said that you cannot offer me any prospects here, Uncle Benjamin, so I must seek them elsewhere,' Henry told him firmly.

'Certainly I could not hold out any hopes of a partnership when your mind is so unsettled,' Uncle Benjamin declared, equally frank with him.

Henry took his law examination in June 1839 and, perhaps even to his own surprise, passed it. He was now a qualified solicitor and he pressed on with his plans for going to Ceylon. By his father's will his mother held £600 for each of her sons. In her generous way she decided to let Henry have his share at once and gave him £300 for the expenses of his journey and arranged for the remaining £300 to be paid into his bank account in Ceylon.

Henry felt rich indeed. £600 was quite a lot of money in

1839. He began to make a plan to go *overland* to Ceylon, by Europe, Central Asia and India, with a short sea-passage to Ceylon. Uncle Charles was able to help him with this plan too. He knew another man who wanted to make an overland journey because he suffered from sea-sickness! He was Edward Mitford, ten years older than Henry and going to Ceylon as a coffee planter. They agreed to be travelling companions on this adventurous journey.

Very few English people had crossed Asia Minor, Persia and Afghanistan to India. Most of the country was unexplored and believed to be inhabited by fierce tribes of wandering bandits ready to rob and murder unprotected travellers. Uncle Benjamin regarded the whole scheme as 'insane' and pointed out all the perils, but Henry was undaunted.

'My mind is made up and nothing can shake my resolution,' he declared.

One person he *did* consult was a friend he had met at the Austen dinner parties, Sir Charles Fellows, famous for his travels and discoveries of ancient Greek cities in Asia Minor. He urged Henry to go and visit parts of Asia Minor yet unexplored. 'I believe there are important ancient ruins still to be found there,' he told the eager young man.

Mitford and Henry Layard planned their route: through Europe to Bulgaria (now Jugo-Slavia), across Turkey to Constantinople, then to traverse Asia Minor with a side-trip to Syria and Palestine, then to Mesopotamia and Baghdad. After that they planned to cross the Persian Mountains to Ispahan, then by way of Yedz and Seistan, exploring as they went. They planned to enter India by the high mountain passes of Afghanistan, then down to the plains of Lahore. After that they would travel the length of India and take ship across the narrow Palk Strait to Ceylon. The Royal Geographical Society had asked them to explore the Seistan district of Persia where few Europeans had been. They were to try to find a new route into India. They reckoned the journey would take them about a year.

It was a breathtaking plan, but Henry was full of confidence. The magic names Constantinople, Jerusalem, Baghdad, Ispahan, rang in his ears like the names in a fairytale. It seemed as if *The Arabian Nights' Entertainments* were about to come true.

With double-barrelled guns, a pair of pistols, compass, sextant, thermometer and barometer and a 'good silver watch painted black so as not to attract thieves', a small medicine chest and a small portmanteau of clothes each, the two young men set out on their high adventure.

On 10th July 1839, exactly a month after Henry had passed his law examination, Henry took ship down the Thames to cross the Straits of Dover to Ostend. He was to meet Mitford at Brussels. As Henry watched London fade astern of the ship in a smoke mist against the setting sun, his thoughts were in a turmoil; he felt sadness at leaving his mother; relief at giving up his dreary work in his uncle's law office; determination to grapple with all the difficulties and dangers that might lie ahead, and joy in the journey awaiting him.

'I was in no way dismayed at the prospect before me', he wrote.

○○

CHAPTER TWO

Journey into Adventure

Henry Layard met Edward Mitford in Brussels and they set off on horses on their long journey eastward. Their route took them through Germany, northern Italy and then to the forested mountains of Montenegro (now Jugo-Slavia). They carried a letter of introduction to the Vladika, the ruling Prince of Montenegro.

As they rode along Henry was thrilled by the colourful appearance of the people. The men wore red embroidered skull caps and jackets adorned with silver ornaments and coins. 'They wear baggy trousers and shave their heads, leaving a kind of pigtail which hangs braided and hung with beads. They carry long guns and wear belts crammed with pistols and knives', he noted in his diary.

The Vladika sent an invitation to visit him at Cettinge, the chief city. Four guides with mules came to conduct them over a rugged and precipitous mountain path.

'They were four savage but fine-looking fellows dressed in short white woollen petticoats (kilts) and a long white woollen cloak and small black turbans and armed to the teeth with pistols and knives', Layard wrote.

The 'palace' at Cettinge was a long white-washed building

of one storey. On a round tower a number of gory heads
were fixed on poles with their long tufts of hair waving in
the wind. They were Turkish heads, cut off by the Montenegrin warriors when they made a raid in Turkey! It was a
shock to Layard and Mitford, but there were more shocks
yet to come.

The Vladika welcomed them in friendly fashion. He was
the tallest man Layard had ever seen, seven and a half feet
high, a perfect giant! He entertained them royally and seemed
quite a civilized person himself. He even had a billiard table,
and that evening they joined him in a game of billiards, but
they were interrupted by loud shouting and the firing of
guns. Montenegrin warriors had returned from a raid on
enemy Turkey. They burst into the room carrying their
offerings in a cloth to the Prince. They emptied it at the
Vladika's feet. Out tumbled a number of bleeding heads!
Among them were those of apparently mere children.
Covered with gore they were a hideous and ghastly spectacle.
'I could not conceal from the Vladika my disgust at what I
witnessed', Layard wrote.

The Vladika agreed that the practice of cutting off their
enemies' heads was shocking and barbarous, but excused it
because it was an ancient custom of the Montenegrins in their
struggle against the Turks.

From Montenegro the two Englishmen went on horseback
to Turkey, staying at Adrianopolis (now Edirne). There they
were stopped and forced to dismount and to enter a kind of
sentry box, completely closed, and to stand on a grating
beneath which was a large pan of sulphur, rosin and other
chemicals, which, when heated, gave off a dense and stifling
smoke. The two men were released half suffocated. This
treatment was given to all travellers, to kill any germs of the
plague they might be carrying.

Layard stayed only long enough in Adrianopolis to visit

the splendid mosque (a Moslem temple), then they continued their journey to the shores of the Sea of Marmora. Here they crossed an arm of the sea, known as the Golden Horn, by a bridge of boats and came to Constantinople (now named Istanbul) and lodged at a small hotel in Pera. Here Henry Layard had his first attack of malaria. For some days he was delirious and very ill. At last he regained enough strength to leave Constantinople. He bought three strong horses accustomed to long journeys and to heavy loads. He also hired a Greek, Giorgio, to act as guide and to cook for them. The journey took them across the narrow strait of the Bosphorus and into Asia Minor.

'We are now about to penetrate into regions untraversed by Europeans and where we would have to rely entirely on

Constantinople in 1839
From a painting by W. H. Bartlett

our own resources, guided by the help of our compass and very imperfect maps', Layard wrote.

They carried with them as little baggage as possible; stockings and boots, waterproof cloaks, blankets and sleeping bags, medicine chest, compass and maps, and above all plenty of powder and shot for their guns.

Layard mapped the route as they went along. He always kept his eyes open for ancient monuments and ruined cities, copying any inscriptions he found. Most of the people were shepherds, much as they are today. Often the two travellers slept on the floors of shepherds' huts or in their tents. They found the Turks honest and hospitable. This is true of the Turks in Asia Minor today, too.

They reached the ancient city of Lystra once visited by Saint Paul, where they found the remains of very old Christian churches. Henry was fascinated by the wall paintings, centuries old. Already the lure of old places held him in thrall.

Their way led over the high passes of the Taurus mountains. Once they spent the night at an encampment of Turcoman families who had just arrived with their flocks. They met with great kindness: wood for a fire was brought to them; they were given a supper of vegetables with a little meat; bread fried in butter; honey and cheese. The shepherds also lent them fine carpets on which to sleep and coverlets for the bitter cold night. Layard remembered this wonderful night for a long time.

'We lay down to sleep', he wrote, 'under a bright starlit sky, the fires of the wanderers burning brightly around us on the mountain sides. About two hours before daylight the whole encampment was ready to move on, loading camels and collecting flocks.'

They reached Tarsus on the Mediterranean shore. They had successfully crossed unexplored Asia Minor by routes

unknown to Europeans. Layard had found the region rich
in historical ruins. He wished he had known more of
archaeology, the study of ancient buildings and monuments.
'By my travels I have learned much', he wrote. The love of
old places was growing strong in him. It was a love which
was to point the way his life was to go.

The two men journeyed on through Syria to Jerusalem.
Though Layard found Jerusalem interesting, it was full of
quarrelling people, and he hated 'the shameful contests
between rival Christians'. He declared he was not sorry when
the time came to leave the city.

At Jerusalem a split developed between Layard and Mitford. Henry could not have enough of the old places and
wanted to make a journey to Petra, a city cut out of red rock,
a city 'half as old as time'. Mitford wanted to push on towards
India. He warned Henry of the Bedouin robbers and
assassins he might encounter.

'I was determined, however, not to be frustrated,' Layard
declared, 'so we agreed to part for a time and to meet again
at Aleppo.'

With Layard went a Christian Arab lad, Antonio. They
joined a wandering Arab tribe whose sheikh or chieftain,
Abu Dhaouk, agreed to lend them a camel and armed men
to lead Layard to Petra. 'But I cannot promise you will be
safe in Petra,' he warned Layard.

At Petra, Layard met a very hostile crowd, unwilling to let
him through the gates into the rose-red city. They threatened
him with knives and stones. Henry knew he was close to
being robbed and having his throat cut, but he stood his
ground boldly. The Arabs with him interpreted what he had
to say.

'If any harm befalls me or these three men of the tribe of
Sheikh Abu Dhaouk, be sure the Sheikh will avenge us. The
Government will order him to do that. They will tell him

he must wipe out the people of Petra or lose his own head.'

The men of Petra talked quietly among themselves. They feared Sheikh Abu Dhaouk.

'I wish only to look at the ruins of your old city and then we will go in peace,' Henry told them.

They gave in with an ill grace and allowed Layard within the gates. They followed him at a distance shouting curses as he walked round their city, but they did not attempt to harm him.

After visiting Petra, Layard journeyed to Kerak, not far from the present capital of Jordan, Amman. In a narrow mountain pass a band of robbers suddenly leaped out on them from behind rocks. They were led by their chieftain. Layard always carried his gun at the ready. At once he boldly raised it and covered the chieftain, threatening him with death if one of his cut-throat band laid a hand on them. He separated the chief from his robber tribe and drove him as a hostage before him. The bandits did not dare to lift a finger against Layard. When they reached the outskirts of Kerak the sheikh of Kerak came out to greet him with a body of men. Only then did Layard let the robber chief go free. His boldness in taking the chief prisoner had saved him and his two Arab companions from certain death.

On the way back to Damascus he was not so lucky. He and Antonio were on foot, trying to ford a flooded mountain stream, when a pack of deserters from the Egyptian army set upon them. They seized Layard and took his money belt and spare clothing and his cloak and gave him a ragged one in its place. Luckily they had no use for his books and papers, nor even his gun as they had no bullets for it, nor his compass. The man who had been leading Layard's mules had made off with them at the first sight of the robbers. Once the thieves had gone, he came back again, but he refused to push on to Damascus for fear he would be seized and pushed into the

The ruins of a temple at Petra
Engraved by W. H. Lizers

army. He found a man in a nearby village, however, who
agreed to take Henry to Damascus and be paid by him after
he had found his friends there. The man insisted that he must
go on foot and by night. Layard knew there was a risk that
he might be attacked and robbed by the guide himself, but
if he did not get to Damascus then he might have to stay for
a long time in the filthy hole of a village and never see
Mitford again. Henry took a chance. The guide proved honest
and after walking for hours in the murky night, wading
through streams and scrambling over rocks and walls, at last
they reached the city gates of Damascus. Here they mingled
with a crowd of farmers bringing vegetables and fruit to the
market. Once inside the walls, Layard made haste to find
Mr Wherry, the British Consul. You can imagine his surprise
when a filthy looking man, clad in a torn Arab cloak and
ragged shirt, smothered in mud and soaking wet, spoke to

him in perfect English and introduced himself as Henry
Layard!

At Aleppo, Layard rejoined Edward Mitford. On the 18th
March 1840, they set out for Baghdad. Layard's heart lifted.
He was on the way to the city of his boyhood dreams.

It was eight months since they had left home and they still
had two-thirds of their journey to go towards Ceylon. They
pushed on and reached Mosul, the great junction of the trade
routes on the west bank of the River Tigris. On the east bank
across from Mosul appeared a line of lofty mounds. These
were the mounds now known to contain the ruins of ancient
Nineveh, the city of the Assyrian kings. He made a further
journey of twenty miles to find Nimrud. In later years
Layard wrote, 'I saw for the first time the great conical
mound of Nimrud rising against the clear sky.' The impres-
sion it made on him was never forgotten.

He also wrote, 'There was a legend among the Arabs that
strange figures carved in black stone still existed among the
ruins but we searched for them in vain during the greater
part of a day in which we were engaged in exploring the
heaps of earth covering a considerable extent of country on
the right bank of the Tigris.'

Those strange figures in black stone were to haunt Layard
for a long time to come. He began to feel the overpowering
urge to dig up this city of the past, but a week later they had
to leave Mosul for Baghdad.

They sailed down the river Tigris on a 'kelek', a raft
floated on inflated goat-skins. The waters of the river were
swollen by the melting snows of the Armenian Mountains
and the raft was washed by the swift current over a mass of
solid masonry. The Arab steersman told them it was the
remains of a great dam built by King Nimrud in ancient
times to hold back the waters and turn them into a network
of canals which then irrigated the land. As they drifted along

the Arab told them stories of kings who once inhabited these
lands and of the palaces supposed to be buried under the
mounds. The glow of the twilight quickly faded away and
night fell suddenly. Before he slept, however, Layard made
a resolve. 'My curiosity had been greatly excited and *from
that time I formed the design of thoroughly examining, whenever
it might be in my power, these strange remains.*'

Layard and Mitford stayed about six weeks in Baghdad.
Here they joined a 'caravan', a company of merchants and
pilgrims on their way to Kermanshah in Persia, travelling
together for protection from bandits.

At Kermanshah their difficulties began. There was strong
dislike of the British at that time in Persia and they were
told they could go no further without special permission
from the Shah of Persia who was encamped with his army
at Hamadan. Over the mountains of Luristan the two men
rode wearily till they reached Hamadan. Here they managed

Damascus from the mountain side

to arrange an interview with the Persian Prime Minister but not the Shah. The Prime Minister refused point-blank to allow them to travel through the province of Seistan. There was a dispute at the time about Seistan, whether it belonged to Persia or Afghanistan, and he was suspicious about the two Englishmen wanting to go there.

Layard and Mitford hung about in Hamadan for several weeks. As they waited for permits to continue their journey, Layard worked hard at learning the Persian language. Mitford was all for going by Bushire on the Persian Gulf on a route that was permitted, but Layard wished to take a different route over the mountains to Isfahan in Persia. Layard decided to 'go it alone', so the two men parted company. Mitford was not sufficiently adventurous for Henry Layard.

Layard carried a letter of introduction to the Metamet, the Governor of Isfahan. Henry asked for a permit to travel through Seistan, but the Metamet would not hear of it. He agreed, however, to allow him to travel through the Bakhtiyari Mountains to Kala Tul on the way to Shushter. This suited Layard quite well for he was 'able to visit a country unexplored by Europeans in which I have been led to suppose I should find important ancient monuments'.

He travelled with a Bakhtiyari leader, Shefir Khan, brother to the chief of the tribe. Layard wore their Bakhtiyari costume. The mountains were full of hostile thieving tribes and even Layard's quilt was stolen as he slept. They were travelling to the castle of Kala Tul, the home of the chief, Taki Khan. When they got there on 5th October 1840, they found the chief was away directing the movements of his flocks from their summer pastures in the mountains to their winter quarters on the plains.

They found the women in the castle in a great state of alarm and grief. The eldest son of the Taki Khan's chief wife was dangerously ill. Layard was thought by the tribesmen

to be a clever doctor because he carried medicines, so the
wife sent for him. He found her weeping and watching over
the child.

'Please save the boy,' she begged. 'He is my eldest son and
dearly loved by his father, Mahommed Taki Khan.'

The boy, about ten years old, was in a very weak state
from malarial fever. Henry gave the mother some doses of
quinine for her to give him. She was afraid of the strange
medicine. Before she would give the quinine to the child she
consulted the 'Mulla' or priest. He consulted the Koran, the
holy book of the Mohammedans, by opening it at random
and reading a passage. The reading was unfavourable and the
Mulla told the woman to give the medicine to the dogs and
to bathe the boy with melon juice and wine instead.

That night was a very hot one and Layard slept in the open
air covered only by a cloak. The next morning the little son
of Taki Khan was worse and his mother brought him to
Layard. He was angry when he heard that she had not given
the medicine to the boy.

'Go consult your Mulla again,' he told her.

'Only save the boy and the Khan will give you splendid
horses and many presents,' she begged him.

Again Layard gave her a dose of quinine. Again she consulted the Mulla as to the best time to give the medicine to
the lad. Once again the Mulla read the Koran and declared
the hour was not favourable. The boy grew steadily worse.

At length Taki Khan returned home. When he saw his
son's state he sent at once for Layard. Sobbing and in deep
distress he cried, 'My son is at the point of death. I will give
you horses or anything you ask if you will only save my
child's life. The doctors of the Bakhtiyari say they can do no
more for him. My only hope is in you. I beg you to save
him.'

'The medicines I left for the boy were never given to him,'

Layard told him sternly. 'Nevertheless I will do all I can to
save his life provided the doctors of your tribe do not
interfere.'

The Khan agreed, but he also consulted the Mulla, who
in his turn consulted the Koran. This time the message from
the holy book was favourable. It was the middle of the night
when Layard was taken to the boy, whom he found in a
high fever. He gave the child a powder to reduce the fever
and decided to stay the rest of the night and watch over him
with the distracted parents. The child broke into a sweat and
the fever began to abate. Layard followed up the powder
with a dose of quinine. The lad fell into a peaceful sleep and
by morning he was much better.

Henry was thankful the child had recovered. If he had
died, the Khan might have blamed Henry. As it was, the
Khan was very grateful and as a reward promised to help
Layard to visit the ruins and monuments in the Bakhtiyari
Mountains.

'If the child had died I might have been accused of poison-
ing him by the native doctors', Layard wrote.

In 1836 Major Rawlinson had written a paper for the
Royal Geographical Society of a march he had made to
Khuzistan and through the province of Luristan. Rawlinson
had mentioned mounds which he thought might conceal the
ruins of ancient cities. Layard now visited these areas and was
able to add to and correct Rawlinson's information. It was
about this time that Layard decided to give up the idea of
going to India and Ceylon. Instead he returned to Kala Tul
after a visit to Kerak, and explored further among the
mountains. He found thirty-four figures sculptured in a rock
foundation with a long inscription below them in wedge-
shaped lettering which he copied.

Taki Khan had refused to pay taxes to the Persian Shah
and he was captured by Persian troops. Layard joined in a

night-attack in an attempt to rescue his friend, but the attempt failed and Layard found himself alone in the mountains. He managed to make his way to Shuster where Metamet, the Governor, put him under open arrest. He was free to stay in his lodging, but he was not allowed to leave the city. The heat was intense, 120 degrees Fahrenheit, but Layard was tough. When the chance came he escaped into the baking heat of the Khuzistan plains and made his way to Basra in late August 1841.

Henry was anxious to return to Baghdad, so he set off on horseback with a messenger employed by the East India Company. On the way they were attacked twice by robbers who took their horses, shoes, clothes, everything except their shirts. Layard's good Arab robe was taken and a dirty ragged one given him in exchange. All that night he and his companion staggered on towards Baghdad, lying sometimes by the roadside to rest. With bare and bleeding feet they at last reached the city gate about sunrise. They were in danger of being turned away as beggars until a number of Englishmen came riding through the gates. Layard recognized one of them. He ran alongside his horse, shouting, 'Doctor Ross! Stop, please!'

The doctor reined in his horse and stared at the filthy beggar who spoke English so well. 'Who are you?' he cried.

'Layard! Henry Layard!'

'Why, bless my soul! It *is* Layard. What on earth have you been doing to yourself?'

Explanations followed and Ross took Layard home and gave him a bath, food and fresh clothes.

In spite of all his adventures Layard was still anxious to go on exploring ancient ruins in Khuzistan and south-west Persia. He thought British merchants might be interested in trading with these lands.

Colonel Taylor in Baghdad wished to inform the British

Ambassador in Constantinople, Sir Stratford Canning, of
affairs in Khuzistan, so he sent a letter by Henry Layard, who
undertook to give Canning a first-hand report on the
country. This time Henry journeyed with a dispatch carrier
of the Turkish government. Business kept the messenger
three days at Mosul, a lucky thing for Henry Layard, and
one of the chances that helped to shape his life. There he met
Paul Emile Botta, the French Consul. Botta was keenly
interested in the study of ruins and ancient monuments in
old cities. When he found Layard was keenly interested in
these things too, he took him to see the trenches he had been
digging in the great mounds of Kuyunjik across the river
Tigris from Mosul. This later proved to be the site of ancient
Nineveh, the capital city of the kings of Assyria. At the time,
though, Botta's digging had turned up little of value and he
had abandoned his work there. Instead he had decided to dig
at Khorsabad, a village fifteen miles away. Layard was deeply
interested. More and more he felt he wanted to stay in this
land of old civilizations.

Layard visited Sir Stratford Canning, the British Ambassador in Constantinople (Istanbul), who liked the young man
and thought he might be useful with his knowledge of the
Bakhtiyari tribes and Persian people. Layard hoped the
British Government would give him a post at the Embassy
at Constantinople, but none was offered. Instead, Canning
employed him unofficially on a mission to Serbia with a view
to retaining the services of this promising young man, so
Henry put off his return to Britain.

In March 1843 came the news of Botta's finds at Khorsabad
of immense sculptured limestone slabs depicting battles and
sieges and the figure of an Assyrian king with a thick, curled
beard and strange head-dress. There was also an inscription
in wedge-shaped (cuneiform) writing. Actually Botta was
uncovering the chief city of Assyria built by King Sargon II

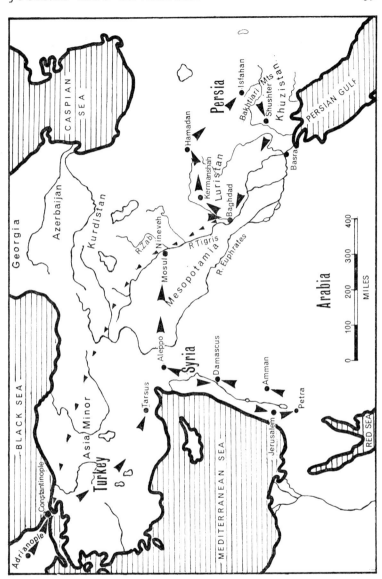

Map of Layard's first journey

around 800 B.C. Botta sent an account of his discoveries to
Henry Layard. Again Layard was fired with ambition to dig
out these ancient cities and he showed Botta's account to
Sir Stratford Canning.

In Baghdad Henry C. Rawlinson had been appointed
Consul. He had been working for some time trying to
decipher the cuneiform inscriptions which kept turning up
at various diggings. Rawlinson was anxious that the French
should not be the only people to discover the ancient sites of
Mesopotamia, but that the British Government should send
people to dig there too. He wrote to Layard: 'I should be
exceedingly glad if the Ambassador and through him the
Government could be induced to take an interest in the
antiquities of this country.'

The upshot was that Canning decided that he himself
would pay Layard's expenses to conduct a 'dig' in Mesopotamia at Nimrud for two to three months. He made one
or two conditions: that Layard was to keep him informed
about his work and the objects he found: in case of success
Layard was to give Canning early and exact information
about his finds and the best method of removing them, with
an estimate of the cost. He warned Layard to keep clear of
strife between the tribes or Persia and to keep on the good
side of the Turkish authorities.

Henry Layard was filled with joy and full of gratitude to
Canning, who promised if Layard's results were good, to try
to persuade the British Government to pay for future 'digs'.
As soon as Layard obtained an official permit from the
Turkish Government to travel to Mosul, he set off from
Constantinople across Asia Minor over the mountains as fast
as horses could carry him. He descended from the high lands
into the valley of the Tigris, galloped over the vast plains of
Assyria and reached Mosul in twelve days.

His great adventure had begun.

OO

The Palace of Nimrud

W hen he reached Mosul, Layard went to see Mohammed Pasha, the Governor of the province, to show him his
letters of introduction from the Turkish Government. He
had heard rumours of the Pasha's cruel harshness and how
he was hated and feared by the people. He found an ugly,
short, fat man with only one eye and ear, a harsh voice and
surly manners. Layard felt he was not a man to be trusted so
he did not tell him the real reason he had come to Mosul.
Instead he pretended he was on a hunting trip.

In his diary Layard wrote: 'On the 8th November 1845,
having secretly procured a few tools, I engaged a mason at
the moment of my departure, and carrying with me a variety
of guns, spears and other formidable weapons, declared I was
going to hunt wild boars in a neighbouring village and floated
down the Tigris on a small raft.' With him went Mr Ross,
a British merchant of Mosul, and Layard's personal armed
servant and a second servant.

The voyage took seven hours from Mosul to Nimrud. At
sunset they landed and walked to the village of Naifa. Not
a light was to be seen, nor was there even the barking of dogs.

'Nothing here but ruins!' Ross said. 'We had better go

back to the raft and spend the night there.'

'Wait! Look at that hovel! I can see fire through a chink. There is someone inside!' Layard exclaimed.

They found an Arab family crouching over the embers, a man, three women and a number of children. They jumped up in alarm at the appearance of strangers.

'They are Europeans!' the man cried in relief, for he had feared robbers. 'Welcome!' he said and spread corn sacks on the ground. 'Be seated, I beg you, sirs.'

The women and children retreated into a corner of the hut and stared at the strangers. The Arab and Layard talked together in Turkish. He told Layard his name was Awad and his tribe had been plundered and scattered by the Pasha.

Layard felt that here was a man he could trust and who might be useful, so he told the Arab he intended to dig in the mounds near by for the ruins of cities. Layard would need workmen and he offered Awad wages to find diggers for him and to superintend them.

Though it was the middle of the night Awad set off for a village three miles away to find men to work at Layard's 'dig' while Layard stayed in his tumbledown dwelling. Layard could not sleep for excitement.

'Visions of palaces underground, of gigantic monsters, of sculptured figures and endless inscriptions floated before me. I fancied myself wandering in a maze of chambers from which I found no outlet.'

His dream was to prove prophetic. He was in an exhausted sleep when he was wakened by Awad. The sun was rising and Awad had returned with six Arabs who agreed to work for Layard for wages. They set off for the mounds of Nimrud where 'the lofty cone and broad mound broke like a distant mountain on the morning sky'.

Right from the start Layard was lucky. On the mounds he found fragments of pottery and bricks inscribed with the strange wedge-shaped cuneiform writing. This convinced him he was searching in the right place for the lost city. Then Awad called to him, 'Sir, I have found something.' He led Layard to where a part of an alabaster slab was sticking up above the soil.

'Dig down carefully. Take care not to damage the slab,' Layard ordered. Both were very excited. It proved to be a large slab of alabaster, a creamy marble-like rock.

'I think we have come on a wall,' Layard declared, and he directed all six men to work carefully round it.

A second slab was uncovered. They continued digging along the same line and found a third slab. Before the day was ended they had found ten slabs which formed a small oblong chamber. Next Henry Layard cleared the dust off the inner face of one of the stones and found an inscription cut in cuneiform writing in the centre of it. Every slab was found to have an inscription carved in the centre. Layard knew from the valuable kind of stone, alabaster, and that there were inscriptions cut in it, that these slabs were not the ruins of a poor village but a chamber in a king's palace. There must be other rooms!

Next day he added five Turcomans to his work force. Half his men he employed in emptying the chamber found the day before and the other half in digging the south-west corner of the mound.

'Before evening,' he wrote, 'I found myself in a room panelled by slabs about eight feet high. The bottom of the chamber was paved with smaller slabs. They were covered with inscriptions on both sides. In the rubbish near the bottom of the chamber I found several objects in ivory upon which were traces of gilding.'

Awad thought Layard was looking for gold and he carefully collected all the fragments of gold-leaf he could find in the rubbish. He mysteriously beckoned Layard aside, then gave him the fragments wrapped in a scrap of paper.

'O Bey (Master), your books were right. Here is gold, sure enough, and please Allah, we shall find it all in a few days.' He was very surprised, even shocked, when Layard told him he was not looking for gold and he could keep the gold-leaf for himself! But Layard knew he had found an honest workman.

Layard continued to dig trenches in different parts of the mound. He hoped to come on sculptures. He knew the Pasha would have been told about his digging and he thought it would be wiser to return to Mosul and tell him what he had found. He was aware the Pasha could make things very awkward for him and prevent him digging.

When he visited the Pasha, Mohammed talked about all kinds of subjects, but he did not question Layard about his digging. Layard knew, however, that the Pasha was craftily trying to trap him, so Henry told him of his excavations. The Pasha, too, thought Layard was looking for gold. Henry managed to satisfy him by offering that the Pasha should have a servant present at the digging to watch. He also offered that the Pasha should have all the gold that might be found. The Pasha, greedy for wealth, then agreed that he could go on digging.

Layard returned to Nimrud on the 19th November. While he had been away his personal servant had continued with the digging and discovered a wall with a doorway. Layard increased the number of his workmen to thirty. The earth was hard, mixed with fragments of stone and pottery and had to be loosened by picks. Only the men from the mountains were strong enough to wield the picks: the Arabs had to be employed to carry away the soil and rubbish in baskets. More walls were uncovered with carved inscriptions, but no sculptures.

Henry lived in a mud hut in a nearby village. The hut was

divided into two parts, one his living quarters, the other a stable for oxen. A wall full of holes divided them. The roof leaked and the winter rains were beginning. Henry wrote, 'I usually passed the night crouched under a rude table which I had constructed.' Even then he was kept awake by the bleating and coughing of sheep and goats in another nearby hut.

On the 28th November they discovered the top of a wall of slabs. Layard directed the workmen to clear away the earth from both sides of the slabs. The first stroke of the pick revealed the top of a 'bas-relief', a shallow sculpture carved on the stone. The Arabs were as excited as Henry was and went on working even during a heavy shower of rain and uncovered two of these sculptured slabs. On each slab were two carvings separated by an inscription.

On the largest was a battle scene showing a chariot drawn by three galloping horses with rich trappings. Three warriors were in the chariot, one clad in a long chain of mail or metal scales, with a bow at full stretch ready to let fly his arrow. Another warrior drove the horses while a third held a circular shield to ward off the arrows of the enemy.

The lower half of the same slab depicted the siege of a castle. A warrior was climbing a ladder placed against the wall. From two turrets soldiers were shooting arrows and casting stones. In the third turret a woman stood with her hand raised as though asking for mercy. The warriors in the chariot and those attacking the wall all wore strange pointed helmets like night-caps. The second slab bore similar battle scenes.

Layard was not long in finding other sculptures. Near the western wall of the buried city the diggers came on several gigantic carved figures. At the south-east corner was a crouching lion. In the centre of the mound they uncovered a pair of gigantic winged bulls which appeared to be at the

entrance to a chamber. Layard only uncovered the upper part
of these sculptures, thinking it wiser to leave them protected
until he could tell Sir Stratford Canning of their discovery
and arrange for their removal. In the meantime he went to
spend Christmas with Major Rawlinson in Baghdad and to
make arrangements for the removal of the sculptures. This
would probably have to be by rafts down the River Tigris
to the Persian Gulf and then a long sea-voyage to Britain.

On his return to Nimrud Layard found more slabs carved
with human figures and flowers. One was a human figure in
a long robe fringed with carved tassels. In the right hand he
carried a pine cone; in the left a kind of hand-bag or basket.
Two great wings rose from his shoulders. The head was that
of an eagle with a long fierce beak and pointed tongue, still
with traces of red paint. A comb of feathers rose from the top
of the head.

'It was evident that I had at length discovered the earliest
palace of Nimrud', Layard wrote with satisfaction.

On the 20th February, when Layard was returning to the
mound after visiting a friendly sheikh, two Arabs came riding
at a gallop towards him. They reined in their horses and cried,
'Hasten, O Bey! The diggers have found Nimrud himself!
It is wonderful but it is true! We have seen him with our
own eyes! There is no God but Allah!'

Layard hastened to the trench. The workmen were standing in it staring at an object they had covered with their
cloaks. They whipped the cloaks off and there was an
enormous human head sculptured in alabaster!

'I saw at once', Layard wrote, 'that the head must belong
to a winged lion or a bull. The expression was calm yet
majestic. I was not surprised that the Arabs had been amazed
and terrified at this apparition. This gigantic head, blanched
with age, might well have belonged to one of those fearful
beings in the legends of their country. One of the workmen,

on catching a first glimpse of the monster, had thrown down his basket and run off towards Mosul as fast as his legs would carry him.'

Layard knew quite well what would happen when the news reached Mosul. Before any folk from Mosul could arrive Layard ordered another trench to be dug due south from the head. He was certain that the head belonged to a winged lion and that there would probably be a pair of them

marking the entrance to a great chamber. Sure enough, before
night fell he came on the second great figure.

Layard was overjoyed. This indeed called for a celebration.
He ordered sheep to be killed and he sent for a troop of
minstrels. The workmen feasted and danced wild Arab dances
nearly all night. Even the women came in crowds with their
children to stare fearfully at the great heads. They declared
that the great heads belonged to idols that Noah had cursed
before the flood! Layard stationed his own body-servant with
a gun to keep everyone out of the trench.

The terrified workman had dashed into the market-place
at Mosul and shouted that Nimrud the King had appeared.
This news soon reached the ears of the Governor. He sent a
message to Layard to treat the heads with respect and to
disturb them no further and to stop digging at once. Layard
went to see him and agreed to stop digging till the excitement
in the town had died down, but he was allowed to let two
men dig along the walls. By the end of March Layard had
found a second pair of winged lions, half human, which
formed the northern entrance into the chamber. These figures
were about twelve feet high and twelve feet long, with great
wings, the carving sharp and fresh. Layard was sure he had
reached the temple of the palace.

Spring had now come to Mesopotamia. The pasture lands
sported fresh green grass and the meadows were jewelled
with flowers. It was not all beauty, however, for the huts
began to swarm with vermin. 'We no longer slept under the
roofs and it was time to follow the example of the Arabs.'
Layard too camped in a tent on the outskirts of Nimrud.

Henry enjoyed those peaceful evenings as he sat in the
entrance to his tent and watched the sun go down. It was the
life he loved. 'The bleating of sheep and lowing of cattle
became louder as the flocks returned from their pastures and
wandered among the tents', he wrote. 'Girls hurried over the

grass to seek their fathers' cattle. Some were coming from the river bearing a pitcher on their heads or shoulders. Sometimes a party of horsemen might be seen slowly crossing the plain, the tufts of feathers which topped their long spears showing darkly against the evening sky. They would ride up to my tent and give me the usual greeting, "Peace be unto you, O Bey!", then driving the ends of their lances into the ground they would spring from their horses and fasten their halters to the still-quivering weapons. Seating themselves on the grass they related deeds of war and plunder until the moon rose and they vaulted into their saddles and took the way of the desert. The plain now glittered with innumerable fires. As the night advanced they vanished one by one until the landscape was wrapped in darkness and silence, only disturbed by the barking of an Arab dog.'

Before Layard could progress any further with his digging he needed the firm permission of the Turkish Government with instructions to the Governor of Mosul and surrounding tribes not to interfere with his excavations. He also needed money from the British Government to help to pay for his work. Sir Stratford Canning promised to give him all the assistance he could with both governments. While Layard waited for the results of this he went on a visit to Sofuk, the Sheikh of the great Arab tribe of Shammar. Henry had an interesting and exciting time with this desert tribe and recorded that 'We soon found ourselves in the midst of wide-spreading flocks of herds and camels. As far as the eye could reach, still the same moving crowd. Long lines of asses and bullocks laden with black tents, huge cauldrons and carpets; infants crammed into saddle bags; mothers with children on their shoulders; boys driving flocks of lambs; horsemen armed with long tufted spears, scouring the plain on their fast steeds; riders urging their camels on with short hooked sticks; highborn ladies seated in strange contrivances on the

camels' humps. Such was the motley crowd through which
we had to wend our way.'

Sofuk gave them a great welcome and lent Layard two
horsemen to guide him to the golden-coloured limestone
ruins of the city of Al-Hather. There Layard took measure-
ments and made plans of the ruined buildings. Then once
more he crossed the desert back to Mosul again and returned
to Nimrud.

During his absence his two men had been clearing rubble
away from the upper part of the chamber where the human-
headed lions had been found. Among the rubbish they found
many copper ornaments, two small terra-cotta ducks and
inscribed tablets of alabaster. They now had to work in the
heat of the summer with the hot winds blowing over the
desert. The grass of the plain was shrivelled and burnt in a
day. Nevertheless the digging went on, though at times they
were almost blinded and suffocated by dust and sand-storms.
Yet more walls were found of sculptured slabs. In the corner
of one chamber was an immense slab of a winged figure with
a three-horned cap, over sixteen feet high. The bracelets and
armlets and even the hilts of daggers were decorated with
the heads of horses, bulls and rams. Under a human-headed
bull Layard found sixteen beautifully-made copper lions, the
largest a foot long, the smallest about an inch in size. Each
had a ring attached to the back and Layard wondered if they
had been used as weights. The slabs showed battle-scenes; a
tower on an island being defended; warriors swimming on
inflated sheep-skins across a river; the siege of a city with a
battering ram on wheels being drawn up to the walls. Other
slabs showed hunting scenes, with a king letting fly an arrow
against a springing lion. Layard remembered that in the Bible
Nimrod was mentioned as 'a mighty hunter'.

One morning just before dawn Layard was wakened by
an Arab. He had brought letters from Mosul. Layard blew

on a small fire of dried camel dung until he had enough light
by which to read. The letter was from Sir Stratford Canning
and it contained a document from the Grand Vizier, the
Sultan's Prime Minister. It was a permit for Layard to continue his digging and to remove any objects he found. Layard
was overjoyed. He could hardly wait for daylight to see the
Pasha of Mosul to show him the Grand Vizier's letter. Now,
at last, Henry would be able to tackle the great mound of
Kuyunjik, believed to be the site of Nineveh. Hitherto he
had left it alone for fear of interference, since it was within
sight of Mosul, and had concentrated on his digging at
Nimrud.

Henry opened trenches at Kuyunjik where the mound was
highest. He found a few fragments of sculpture and bricks
bearing the name of a king which he could not decipher
properly. After digging there for about a month Layard gave
up the unsuccessful search and returned to Nimrud which
had proved much more rewarding.

At Nimrud Layard employed thirty Arabs to dig in the
north-west palace. There they uncovered a remarkably long
room, a hall 154 feet long but only 33 feet wide. There he
found a very elaborate slab 14 feet in length. On it were
carved two kings standing face to face with a tree between
them. Their hands were raised in prayer. Each king was
followed by a winged figure carrying a fir-cone and a basket.
This carved slab is now to be seen in the British Museum.

The great hall opened into other chambers all panelled in
sculptured slabs. One showed a king seated on a stool-like
throne, holding a cup in his right hand. His servant stood
behind and fanned him with a palm-leaf fan. Beautiful
embroideries were carved on the borders of the kings' and
priests' garments. Assyria was famed for its beautiful cloth
and embroidery. Robes such as these are mentioned in the
Bible as 'the dyed attire and embroidered work', garments

of the kings of this country. This was confirmed by the sculptured bas-reliefs that Layard found: the King wore gorgeous robes adorned with fringes and tassels, necklaces and bracelets; his hair fell in ringlets and his beard was elaborately plaited: above it all he wore a conical, jewelled head-dress.

The Arabs marvelled at the strange figures they dug up. 'They soon felt as much interest as I did in the discoveries,' Layard said, 'and worked with renewed ardour when their curiosity was aroused by the appearance of a fresh sculpture. They rushed like madmen into the trenches to carry off baskets of earth, shouting the war-cry of their tribe.'

Layard was anxious to send to Britain such sculptures as he could move. He asked help from Major Rawlinson in Baghdad who had been working on deciphering the cunei-form inscriptions. A small steamer, the *Nitocris*, was sent up the river Tigris, but her engines were not sufficiently power-ful to carry her up the rapids and she had to return to Baghdad.

Layard was faced with a problem. He had to lessen the weight of the slabs if they were to be carried down-river. He did this by sawing double-panelled carvings into two pieces and by cutting away the back of some of the slabs and 'thinning' them. Unfortunately, by doing this he had to cut away some of the inscriptions on the back, but he said the same inscription was carved on many slabs and so he did not consider it necessary to preserve them all. For this he has been blamed by archaeologists in later years, but it must be remembered he had not the tools nor the equipment in 1846 that they afterwards possessed. 'With the help of levers of wood,' he wrote, 'I was able to move the sculptures into the centre of the trenches where they were reduced (in weight). They were then packed and transported from the mound in buffalo carts to the river where they were placed on a raft constructed of inflated skins and beams of poplar wood. They were floated down the Tigris as far as Baghdad and there transferred to boats.'

They reached the Persian Gulf in August. This was the first collection of Layard's finds to be sent to the British Museum.

Layard's health suffered from the intense heat of the summer and from his many hours in the trenches with hot desert winds like blasts from a furnace sweeping over him. For a week he stayed in underground rooms in Mosul, then set off on a journey among the cooler high mountains of Tiyari. There he found a great welcome and kind hospitality among the Kurdistan tribes. In the valleys he found mines of iron, lead and copper being worked by the natives. Layard made notes of all that he saw and later wrote an account of the country and people in a book.

Assyrians crossing a river on inflated goatskins
From a drawing by A. H. Layard

CHAPTER FOUR

○○○

The Digging Goes On

Henry Layard returned to Mosul in September 1846 to find letters awaiting him from England. Sir Stratford Canning had presented the sculptures Layard had found to the British Museum. He had done his best to arouse interest in Layard's digging at Nimrud. The result was that the British Museum made a grant of £2,000 to Layard to continue his work. It was really a miserably small amount, far less than Botta received from the French Government for his excavations. All the same, Henry Layard took on the job.

'I determined to accept the charge, to make every exertion, to economize as far as it was in my power, that the British nation might possess as extensive and complete a collection of Assyrian antiquities it was possible to collect', he wrote.

He was disappointed too that the British Museum had not sent out an artist to assist him in making records, particularly of those sculptured stones which could not be moved. 'I made up my mind to do the best I could,' he said, 'to copy as carefully and accurately as possible all the bas-reliefs discovered.'

It was a terrific task, for he had to superintend the work of the diggers, even to remove earth carefully from the face of the slabs himself and to supervise their packing and transport. To send out helpers from England would eat up the greater part of his £2,000 before the digging even began, so he decided to carry on alone.

Layard organized a band of workmen from wandering Arab tribes who encamped round the ruins of Nimrud and served also to protect the digging from thieves. He also hired a skilful marble-cutter and a carpenter. It was nearing the end of October and the first thing to be done was to build huts of mud bricks dried in the sun so that Layard and his workers could be housed during the winter rain showers.

'Unfortunately the showers of rain fell before my walls were covered in and so saturated the bricks that they did not become dry before the following spring.' The consequence was that his rooms were constantly clothed in a crop of grass!

Layard began digging at Nimrud on 1st November 1846. Because he had to make the most of what money he had, Layard dug trenches along the sides of the walls as he had done before, without digging in the centre of the chambers. 'Thus few of the chambers were fully explored and many objects of great interest may have been left undiscovered', he wrote.

He dug up more slab carvings that depicted the wars of the king and the conquering of a foreign castle. Neighbouring slabs showed the return after the victory with several warriors throwing down the heads of enemies at the king's feet in the procession of victory. There were some interesting river scenes showing boats very like those still in use on the Tigris in Layard's day, proving that river traffic had altered very little in three thousand years. Men at that time blew up sheep-skins to support themselves as they swam across the river, just as they still did in 1846.

Layard began to find other things beside slabs: scales of

iron; copper armour; a perfect, pointed helmet; broken vases of fine white alabaster, and one or two small perfect ones, each bearing the name and title of the king. They continued digging the trench in the same direction, but nothing new appeared. Layard decided that since they did not seem to be making new discoveries he would go to Mosul on business. All the same he gave instructions to his workmen to go on digging the trench till he came back.

Hardly had he mounted his horse and left the mound than a corner of black marble was uncovered at the very edge of the trench. The foreman ordered the workmen to dig it out. It turned out to be an obelisk about six feet six inches high, lying on its side. At once an Arab was sent to bring Layard back again.

Layard descended eagerly into the trench and realized at once the value of the discovery. The obelisk was sculptured on all four sides with twenty bas-reliefs showing the king. His servants were leading various animals as tribute to him: the elephant, the rhinoceros, the two-humped camel, the bull, the stag, and various kinds of monkeys. Above and below the sculptures were carved inscriptions in cuneiform writing. Layard knew that once Major Rawlinson had completed his studies of this writing, the inscription could be deciphered. Then some of the history of this wonderful ruined city would be revealed. Henry was anxious to get it to London, but first he took the precaution of copying the inscriptions and drawing the carvings on the obelisk. It was then carefully packed and transported by raft down the river to Baghdad. It is now in the British Museum. When the inscriptions were deciphered much later, it was found that one of the figures was that of the messenger of Jehu, King of Israel, doing homage for Jehu to the King of Assyria.

During November and December Layard's digging prospered well. Every day brought some new discovery to light.

'I rose at daybreak,' Layard wrote, 'and after a hasty breakfast rode at once to the mound. Until night I was engaged in
drawing the sculptures, copying and moulding the inscriptions and superintending the excavations and the removal
and packing of the bas-reliefs. On my return to the village
I was occupied till past midnight in comparing the inscriptions with the paper impressions, in finishing drawings and
in preparing the work of the following day.'

It was truth to say he never had an idle moment and,
indeed, little time for sleep.

Layard had collected enough carved slabs for another cargo
to be sent by raft down the Tigris to Baghdad. He bought
wooden spars and sheepskins in Mosul to construct a new
large raft, and also mats and felts for packing the precious
sculptures. These were floated down the river on a smaller
raft to Nimrud. It was late at night when the raftmen reached
the river dam, so they left the raft tied up to the bank. In the
night it was plundered by thieves who made off with the
ropes and felts. Layard knew he would have to act promptly
and firmly or there might be other thefts. He made discreet
inquiries among the people and found that the robbers were
an Arab tribe at a little distance from Nimrud. They were
well known for their thieving of cattle. Layard was determined to teach them a lesson.

At dawn he set off with Ibrahim Agha, his chief foreman,
and another horseman. They reached the Arab encampment
after a long ride. Layard boldly made for the Sheikh's tent
and sat down before it. He was amused to see the women
bustling about the encampment trying to hide the felts and
ropes that had been stolen.

'Peace be unto you!' Layard addressed the Sheikh, with
the customary politeness. 'We are friends and I know the
laws of friendship. My property is your property and your
property is mine. But there are a few things such as mats,

felts and ropes which I need and which can be of little use to you. You will greatly oblige by giving these things back to me.'

The Sheikh wore a guilty look, but declared, 'O Bey, no such things as mats, felts or ropes were ever brought to my tents. Search, and if such things be found we will give them to you willingly.'

'True! The Sheikh has spoken the truth!' all his tribe cried, but Layard knew they were lying, for he had seen one of his new ropes supporting the tent pole!

'I will find the truth, and as this is a matter of doubt the Pasha of Mosul must decide between us,' Layard told the Sheikh.

Henry made a quick sign to Ibrahim who had been waiting for it. In a moment he handcuffed the Sheikh and, jumping on his horse, dragged the Arab after him out of the encampment. The Arabs were all taken by surprise. Layard calmly mounted his own horse.

'I have found a part of what I wanted; you must search for the rest,' he told the tribesmen.

Ibrahim, his pistol in his hand, forced the Sheikh to mount his horse in front of him and off they went at a brisk pace. The tribe set up a wail when they saw their Chief being carried off. Though they were armed the Arabs did not dare to fire for fear of hitting their own Sheikh. Layard joined Ibrahim and they rode off with the kidnapped Sheikh.

The Sheikh had no wish to be taken before the Pasha in Mosul. Too many of the people in the villages would come forward and tell the Pasha how he and his men had robbed them of donkeys, horses, sheep and even a copper kettle. Layard knew this and played on the Sheikh's terror by describing the cellar prison at Mosul and the beatings that thieves received. By the time they reached Nimrud the Sheikh was terrified. He admitted the things had been stolen.

'O Bey, only let me go and I will see that all your possessions are restored to you,' he begged.

Layard pretended he was determined to take him to the Pasha, then he let the Sheikh's agonized pleas appear to make him relent.

'Very well! You will send an Arab to your tents to bring back my belongings. When every single thing is restored to me, then I will let you go. Till then you will be my prisoner.'

The Sheikh sent a messenger to his encampment. All night he groaned in misery till the next morning donkeys appeared before Layard's dwelling. On their backs were tied the missing mats, felts and ropes. As well as the stolen goods they brought a lamb and a kid as an offering of penitence and friendship! After Layard had checked his property he gave the Sheikh a scolding, then let him return to his tribe.

Layard had no more trouble after that with thefts by Arab tribes in his neighbourhood. The story was told around and from then on the Arabs treated Layard with great respect.

It had been a very dry spring and summer in Assyria. The young barley and wheat was burned up as soon as they struggled through the earth. This meant famine later on. The hills were barren of grass and there was no pasture for the sheep. The Bedouins, tribes of wandering shepherds, made sudden swoops on villages to plunder them. The thieving grew worse as the Bedouins grew hungrier and bolder. Layard began to fear that his excavations might be raided and that the large sculptures he had found would be damaged. He determined to try to get a lion and a bull removed and sent down the Tigris on a raft. This was a difficult undertaking because of the tremendous weight of the sculptures.

First Layard had to build a strong cart to carry them down to the river. A carpenter had to be sent to the mountains to find trees with hard, strong wood. At the French consulate Layard found a pair of iron axles which had been used by

Botta in moving sculptures. He purchased these. The cart was an object of wonder to the inhabitants and crowds came to look at it.

Before Layard could even get the carved human-headed bull slab from the ruins, he had to cut a road two hundred feet long and about fifteen feet wide to the entrance of the chamber where the bull stood. This road-making employed fifty Arabs. As they dug they came on yet another chamber where a spirited carving of a lion hunt was found. This too is now in the British Museum.

The sculpture was wrapped in mats and felts: rollers were made of the trunks of poplar trees and laid before it; thick ropes were fastened round the carving and passed through blocks on the ground. The ends of the ropes were held by strong teams of diggers. A tribe of Arabs came to help too. The earth was then dug out below the bull which was supported by beams and wedges. When all was ready Layard gave the signal to pull away the beams and wedges very gradually while the teams of men took the weight of the bull on the ropes. It was a tense moment. The Arabs were frantic with excitement as they clung to the ropes. The women crowded on the sides of the trench and screamed and yelled encouragement. Layard was unable to make himself heard to shout instructions. The bull began to descend towards the rollers: the ropes creaked and stretched more and more. Water was thrown over them. When the bull was about four feet above the rollers the ropes all broke together! The bull fell to the ground! A sudden shocked silence fell on the noisy crowd.

Layard rushed down into the trench expecting to find the bull in fragments. To his surprise it was quite uninjured and lying just where he wanted it across the rollers. When Layard raised his hands in relief and delight a shout of joy went up. The Arabs dashed out of the trench, seized the women by

the hands and quickly making a large circle they commenced
a wild mad dance of rejoicing. Nothing more could be done
till the Arabs had worn themselves out. As soon as they were
ready to resume work wooden sleepers were laid over the
earth in the trench road to take the weight of the bull. New
ropes were fixed round the carving and it was pulled forward
on to the rollers. The sun was going down and work had
to be stopped for the day.

That night there was a feast. The Sheikh Abdurrahman
dined with Layard and for the first time in their lives the
Arabs used knives and forks instead of eating with their
fingers.

'Tell me, O Bey, what are you going to do with these
stones?' the Sheikh asked Layard. 'So many thousands of
purses spent on such things! You say your people will learn
knowledge from them, but these figures will not teach you

Layard supervising the lowering of the great winged bull
From Layard's Monuments of Nineveh

to make better knives or scissors or cloth. It is in the making of those things that the English show wisdom. But God is great! Here are stones which have been buried since the time of Noah. I have lived on these lands for years and my father and his father before me but they had never heard of these figures. For twelve hundred years my tribe has been settled in this country and none of them ever heard of a palace underground. But lo! you come to this very place and with a stick make a line here and a line there. "Here", you say, "is the palace. And here is the gate." You show us what has been all our lives beneath our feet without our having known anything about it. Wonderful! Wonderful! Is it by magic you have learned these things?'

Indeed it seemed a wonder, even to Layard himself, that a stranger should discover monuments that had been buried for more then two thousand years.

The great carved bull was now ready to be dragged over the rollers to the end of the trench. The Arabs hauled on the ropes with a will. When the bull was near to the bottom of the mound the men dug enough earth away to admit Layard's cart. Gradually, while they hung on to the ropes, they allowed the bull to slide from the mound to the cart. The next step was to pull the cart to the river.

Buffaloes were harnessed to the cart, but when they felt the dead weight they refused to move. Animals know how much their strength will endure. The Arabs were forced to unyoke them and in parties of eight the men pulled on the yoke pole in turn while other Arabs hauled on the ropes attached to the cart. The cart began to move slowly.

It was quite a procession! Layard rode at the head of it with his personal servant. Next came a kind of band of drums and fifes playing with might and main to encourage the men. Three hundred men came next dragging the cart, all shouting at the tops of their voices, urged on by their leaders. Behind

the cart the women followed in a crowd screeching encouragement. Arab horsemen dashed round the procession
waving their spears.

All went well till they reached the ruins of a former village.
The villagers stored their corn and barley in deep pits for
the winter. The corn-pits had long been emptied of their
stores but the holes remained, covered by boughs which had
been plastered over by mud. The sand and dust had drifted
over them. Into one of these holes two wheels of the cart
sank. The Arabs pulled and yelled, but the cart could not be
stirred and the ropes broke. The dusk came down and the
cart had to be left there for the night.

Layard feared that the thieving Bedouins might make off
with the ropes and felt mats round the bull, so he decided to
leave a guard of workmen. Sure enough, in the night he
heard the crack of guns and the war-cries of the Bedouins.

Dragging the bull to the river with the mounds of Nimrud in the background
From Layard's Monuments of Nineveh

He rushed to the spot with more men and the robber tribe made off into the desert, but not before a bullet had dented the side of the bull.

Next morning the men levelled out the earth sides of the pit and put thick planks under the buried wheels of the cart. They hauled and shouted furiously and at last the cart moved forward out of the hole. On they went towards the river, but their troubles were not over. On the river bank the wheels sank down into the sand. It took nearly a day's work to dig them out and put planks beneath the wheels. At last the bull was hauled on to a low platform constructed by the river. From the platform the bull was to be slid on to the raft that was to carry it down the river.

Again Layard left a guard over the bull and went through the same performance to bring the sculptured lion down to the waterside. This time he doubled the ropes and the number of men hauling on them. Even then the cart sank several times in the sandy soil. After two days, however, it stood beside the bull on the banks of the Tigris.

Now Layard encountered labour troubles. He had sent other lighter sculptured slabs only as far as Baghdad, where they had been transferred to small, frail boats built by natives. These boats carried them down to Busrah where they were transferred to ocean-going ships that could come up with the tide. This time Henry did not wish to risk his heavy sculptures being lifted from the rafts to poor frail craft at Baghdad. He asked the raftmen of Mosul to take the sculptures all the way to Busrah. This they refused point blank to do. They said their rafts could not carry such heavy burdens. As usual, Layard found a way out of the difficulty.

In Baghdad there was a man, Mullah Ali, who was willing to build a raft big enough to take the sculptures. The raft was made of logs bound together with willow twigs. The skins of sheep and goats were dried and prepared and made

into bags with just one opening. These bags were inflated
like balloons by air being blown into them. Once they were
fully inflated the opening was quickly tied up and the bag
was fastened to the under side of the raft by more twigs.
The skins were placed with the opening upwards so they
could easily be blown up again. Then the raft was launched.
Layard knew the skins would have to be inflated again once
they reached Baghdad to carry them on to Busrah and he
made arrangements for this to be done.

It would be easier to row the rafts down the river when
there had been a slight flood. On the 20th April, 1847, the
Tigris rose slightly with the spring rains. Labourers cut away
the high bank of the river into a steep slope. The raft was
then brought opposite the bull and the sculpture was let down
gradually on to the raft by ropes. Next the lion was embarked
in similar fashion. Mullah Ali kissed Layard's hand, settled
down on the raft and slowly floated with its precious burden
down the river.

Layard stood on the bank and watched them go till they
reached a bend in the river and were hidden from sight. He
thought of how they had adorned the palace of the Assyrian
kings and had laid buried for centuries, unknown, while great
kings had fought wars on the soil above them. Now they
had set off on a long sea-journey to lands which were not
even known when busy hands had carved them. At last, their
travels over, they would reach the British Museum.

It was a good thing that Layard got his treasures away
when he did. The friendly tribe of Arabs, the Abou-Salman,
who had helped him to dig and to load his rafts, left the
countryside to find fresh pastures for their flocks. The
Bedouins increased their thieving raids and Layard had to
arrange for patrols of his workmen to watch over his property
at night.

'I was roused almost nightly by shouts and the discharge

of firearms when the whole encampment was thrown into commotion,' he wrote.

The Bedouins grew bolder. They attacked a settlement within sight of Nimrud, murdered several inhabitants and drove away the sheep and cattle. Layard's workmen feared to stay any longer in the neighbourhood. Henry decided it was time to stop digging. He had been instructed by the British Museum to cover up again any sculptures he had not been able to remove. Accordingly his labourers carried back the earth and heaped it over the slabs and walls till the palace was buried again. The wonderful sculptures were once more concealed from the eye of man and Nimrud was desolate once more, the ancient city vanished like a dream.

'Some, who may hereafter tread on the spot where the grass again grows over the ruins of Assyrian palaces, may indeed suspect that I have been relating a vision', Layard wrote sadly.

The treasures that reached the British Museum, however, proved that the discoveries were no dream.

Henry Layard still had some money left from the grant the British Museum had made so he decided to investigate the mound of Kuyunjik right opposite Mosul across the Tigris. He was encouraged to do this because his friend Botta, the French archaeologist, had done some digging on this mound and had already found some sculptured slabs. Botta ceased digging there, however, when he found the ruins had been badly damaged by fire and he went instead to Khorsabad. Layard thought that further digging might reveal more secrets of the mound. Another reason for his decision was that the people of the nearby city of Mosul would serve to protect his labourers from marauding Bedouin tribes. Reports had also been made to him that carved stones had been found when people had dug into the mound to obtain building materials.

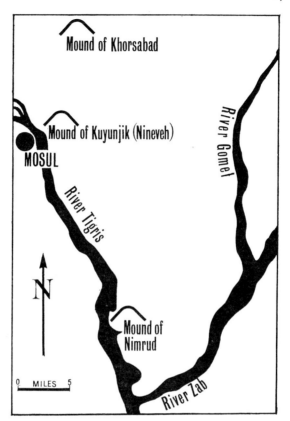

Layard also wanted to test his theory that the mounds of Nimrud, Kuyunjik and Khorsabad had once formed part of one great city with a palace-temple at the centre of each district. These palace-temples had great parks with walls built round them and probably there were mud huts to house the people also within the walls, as well as orchards and gardens.

Layard had been reading the book of Jonah in the Bible and Jonah had described Nineveh as 'an exceeding great city of three days' journey' to ride round its walls. Layard reckoned the distance round the mounds was about sixty miles. A distance of twenty miles is reckoned a day's journey by the desert tribes and it would therefore take three days to encircle the ancient city which, at the time of Jonah, housed about 120,000 people.

Henry believed that the first city with its palace-temple was built by Nimrud. This was where he dug first. The other palaces were built by kings of a later age. It might be asked, 'What happened to the homes of the people? Why are only the *palaces* found?' The answer is that the houses were probably built of mud bricks dried in the sun. During the passage of time these bricks crumbled and fell into dust and could not be distinguished from the earth on which they were built. The only stone to be found in the area of the plains was marble-like alabaster, so this was reserved for building the palaces. This alabaster survived the ravages of time.

It was in the middle of May 1847 when Layard quitted Nimrud. He set to work at once on the mound of Kuyunjik. Botta had dug pits to try to find sculptures but with very little luck. Layard decided the best plan was to dig trenches towards the highest part of the mound where the temple was most likely to be.

The workmen dug for some days without finding anything but some fragments of burnt alabaster. Layard left them to go on with the work while he went shopping in Mosul. As he came out of the market two Arab women came running up to him, their dresses soaked with water.

'O Bey, a sculpture has been uncovered!' they cried with joy. 'As soon as the diggers had uncovered the first slab we rushed to cross the river to tell you. We did not even wait to come by the bridge, but we blew up sheep-skins and swam across on them. That is why our clothes are still so wet. We came at all speed, O Bey!'

They knew that Layard always made a good present to the first bearer of good tidings of a 'find'. He did not disappoint them, but hardly had he pressed the money into their eager palms than a man came pounding up to them. He was Toma Shishman, 'Fat Toma' as he was called, one of Layard's chief overseers. He had hardly breath left to gasp the news of the find into Layard's ears. Toma had come by the bridge but the wily women had beaten him by boldly swimming the river.

Layard returned at once to the ruins. He found the workmen had uncovered a wall and an entrance to a chamber. They dug along the wall and found more winged bulls. They also found fragments of pottery and small glass bottles. By the time a month had passed nine long, narrow chambers had been explored. Much of the palace had been destroyed by fire but the diggers found sculptured slabs much larger than those found at Nimrud. There were more winged human-headed bulls. Some inscribed tablets also proved Layard's theory that the palaces have been built at different periods by kings of the same family.

The carved slabs again depicted battle scenes. They showed burning houses, soldiers marching in regiments carrying shields and spears. There were triumphal processions of warriors returning with captives and loot. One carving showed a castle with the king receiving chained prisoners with spoil from the captured cities.

Layard guessed that the sculptures might picture the siege and conquest of Tyre or Sidon, for there were interesting scenes of ships and the sea. He thought the king might be Sennacherib, famous in Byron's poem *The Assyrian Came Down like a Wolf on the Fold*. The vessels might be those of the Phoenicians who coasted along the shores of the Mediterranean and entered the Atlantic Ocean, even reaching Britain.

There was a magnificent slab showing the king standing in his chariot, holding a bow in his left hand and raising his right hand as though saluting his people. Over his head a slave held an open sunshade. The chariot was drawn by two horses and before it went spearmen and archers.

The inside of these Assyrian palaces must have been truly magnificent, the entrances guarded by enormous stone lions or bulls. The stories of kings, battles, sieges and triumphs were carved on the alabaster slabs forming the walls. Most of these were painted in bright colours. At the end of the great hall stood an enormous sculpture of the king in gorgeous painted robes. No wonder the early writers spoke of the 'glory of Nineveh'.

By the middle of June 1847 Henry Layard had spent all the money the British Museum had allowed him and some of his own savings as well. He had been eight years in the Near East and Assyria, working in exhausting heat, living rough with the Arabs, travelling by foot and on horseback thousands of miles. His health was beginning to suffer and he was very tired. He decided it was time he turned his steps homeward. Once more his excavations were covered up and the palaces hidden.

Looking back on his work, Henry Layard felt a sense of satisfaction. The sculptures were on their way to the British Museum: the inscriptions on others had been carefully copied: Rawlinson at Baghdad was busy deciphering them and soon the lost history of this ancient country and fabulous cities would be given to the world. Scarcely a year before nothing had been known of these wonderful buried monuments that proved the existence of great Nineveh.

It was not without sadness that Layard parted with his loyal workmen of the Jebour tribe. Before he left he gave a great party to them and their families, with huge plates of rice and mutton, and he made presents to them all.

'Please God I shall return to the Jebours and live in tents with them on their pasture grounds', Henry wrote in his diary.

When he left Mosul all the chief residents rode with him out of the town. Beyond the bridge were his workmen with their wives and families. They clung to his horse, kissed Layard's hand and shed tears. Many of the men walked alongside him till nightfall to the village of Tel Kef where they had supper and talked round the fire till midnight. The horses were again loaded and saddled and Layard bade a last farewell to his Arabs and set off on the road to Constantinople. Not even an Assyrian king had been so loved and respected by his people.

○○

The Great Library of Nineveh

Henry Layard reached England on the 22nd December 1847, just in time to eat his Christmas dinner with his mother and relations. He had been away eight and a half years. He found he was no longer an unknown man. In June the first consignment of the sculptured slabs had reached the British Museum. Their display aroused great interest, not only in themselves but in the young man who had found them. His mother was immensely proud of him. Even Uncle Benjamin Austen forgot how he had discouraged Henry from his journey into adventure and welcomed him as the guest of honour at his dinner table. The University of Oxford awarded Layard an honorary degree. How often had Henry longed to go to Oxford when he was an apprentice to his uncle, drearily studying law in a cold office by candlelight!

Soon after his return home Layard wrote to the British Museum urging them to go on with digging in Mesopotamia. He was sure there were many sites of ancient cities that would yield treasure. He warned the authorities that quick action was needed, for other nations were only too ready to step in and go on digging where he had left off. Money was urgently required for the work. He suggested that the British Museum might ask the Government for a grant of £4,000 to carry on the work for a year. The Government could not see its way to do this. There was revolt in India and the continent was very unsettled. Possibly its funds might be needed for more urgent matters.

Layard was a very disappointed man. He became gloomy and ill as he thought that all his hard work was going for nothing. He found sympathetic friends in his cousin, Lady Charlotte Guest, and in her husband, Sir John Guest, and he visited them frequently. They encouraged him to write a book about his travels. With the writing of it his spirits began to rise. He had to work at great speed, for he had neither much time nor money. In spite of bouts of malarial fever he worked hard on the two volumes of *Nineveh and Its Remains*, telling of his travels and of his digging for the ancient palaces. A publisher, John Murray, had it printed.

In October the fifty cases Layard had sent from Nimrud arrived at the British Museum after their journey half round the world. The ship in which they came had almost foundered in a gale off Ceylon. What priceless treasures might have been lost!

Layard was present at the British Museum when the cases were opened. Imagine his shock and horror to find some of the smaller objects were broken; others were missing and the whole collection was out of order. The catalogue he had made of the ivories, copper vessels and vases, giving details of the places where they had been found, was now useless. The finds had been hastily and carelessly repacked. Layard was livid with anger. He and the authorities of the British Museum were determined to find out who had interfered with his carefully packed cases.

The trouble was traced to Bombay. There, while the cases had been waiting in the Customs' House to be shipped to England, the British residents were so full of curiosity that they persuaded the Customs' officers to open the cases to

examine the contents. The precious finds had been passed
from hand to hand and one or two people had even helped
themselves to the small articles they fancied! A clergyman
in Bombay had even opened up the most precious of Layard's
finds, the famous Black Obelisk of King Shalmaneser, and
had dared to give a sermon on it! Afterwards they had repacked the treasures so carelessly that many of them were
damaged on the way. People in Britain were so shocked at
this report that the whole business became a national scandal.
One good result came of it. Afterwards, cases that were
addressed to the British Museum received very careful
handling and protection on the way.

Layard was anxious to go back to Turkey again and resume
his digging. He was offered a post, unpaid, in the British
Embassy in Constantinople (Istanbul). He was dismayed that
no money from the Government was promised to help with
his excavations. Soon his fortunes were to change.

In February 1849 his book was published. It took the
reading public by storm. *The Times* newspaper gave it a
glowing review and called it 'the most extraordinary work
of the present age'. It praised Layard's 'brave spirit and noble
aim'. What was more, though, it added: 'We wish it was in
our power to add that the Government has adequately
rewarded the man who has sacrificed his health and, with
unwearied energy and courage, devoted his high talents to
our service, enriching our national museum with such
splendid remains. But we are sorry to be obliged to inform
our readers that Mr Layard has had no reward.' *The Times*
also told the public that Layard had been appointed to an
unpaid position in the British Embassy in Constantinople and
pointed out too that one of his sculptures was still lying on
a raft in the mud at Busrah waiting to be shipped to England.

The Times article raised a storm of indignation. Public
feeling was stirred and the Government was strongly

criticized. As a result, in April 1849 Layard was offered a
paid post at the Embassy at Constantinople. The Treasury,
through the British Museum, offered £3,000 to be spent on
digging in Mesopotamia, half of it to last until May 1850.

Henry was disappointed with the amount so grudgingly
given. He wrote to Sir Henry Ellis, the Trustee of the British
Museum, pointing out the expenses of the journey to Mosul,
the cost of supplies, the wages of the workmen and the high
charges for shipping to England the sculptures he had found.

'It is hardly prudent on my part to embark on a second
expedition with such very limited means at my disposal, but
as the Trustees [of the Museum] have reckoned on my
services, I will not raise difficulties at the last moment.'

He was so keen to carry on with digging out his lost cities
that he even offered his own salary of £150 to help with the
work.

In October 1849 he returned to Mosul, taking with him
an artist, Frederick C. Cooper, to help with the copying of
the inscriptions and small drawings, and a physician, Dr H.
Sandwich, and Hormudz Rassam, his Turkish assistant and
friend.

On the way to Mosul they stopped at an Arab encampment
to ask for water. The Arabs were the Jebours who had worked
before for Layard at Nimrud. They danced round him in joy.

'O Bey, we heard you were to come again to dig for old
stones. We were on our way to join you at Nimrud,' they
cried.

Further along the road they found 'Fat Toma', his former
foreman, waiting for them with Behnan the stone-cutter,
and Hanna the carpenter. A feast was awaiting Layard at Tel
Kef. The word had gone before him and next morning
Layard was welcomed by sheikhs of the Jebour who rode
out to meet him. One even brought Henry's horse, Meijan,
'looking as beautiful, fresh and sleek as when I saw him two

years ago', Layard wrote in his diary.

Layard was deeply touched, almost to tears, by the devotion of 'his' people.

'Old servants take their places as a matter of course and uninvited pursue their regular occupations as if they had never been interrupted.'

It was a homecoming that made him feel warm at the heart. His spirit lifted as he saw the vast mound of Kuyunjik overtopping the surrounding heaps.

Once more Layard resumed his excavations at Nimrud. He was pleased to find that most of the sculptures he had covered up had not been damaged by Bedouin gangs.

By the end of November they dug out a large hall. Here the carved pictures on the alabaster walls depicted a war, with the foes having their heads struck off. The next sculpture saw the heads being heaped at the feet of the king! Groups of captives were being marched along and the carvings pictured their national dresses and headgear. From these carvings we know how many of the nations dressed who lived in the countries bordering on Assyria.

The sculptures on the north side of the room interested Layard very much indeed. They showed how the Assyrians had moved the great stone sculptures. They had done it then exactly as Layard had organized it 2,500 years later. They had worked with rollers and levers, ropes and hundreds of men. The long lines of slaves, whipped on by overseers, pulled the great blocks of stone on a large sledge, watched by the king. There was an inscription which read, 'Sennacherib, King of Assyria, transported thither the great figures of bulls which were made for his royal palace at Nineveh'.

Undoubtedly Layard had found the palace of Sennacherib, the king mentioned in the Bible as making war on Hezekiah, King of Judah. Sennacherib had recorded on the carved stones, 'Hezekiah, King of Judah, who had not submitted to my authority, forty-six of his principal cities and fortresses I captured'.

In the Bible it states: 'Now in the fourteenth year of King Hezekiah did Sennacherib, King of Assyria, come up against all the fenced cities of Judah and took them.'

Another slab described Sennacherib as 'The subduer of kings from the upper sea of the setting sun [Mediterranean] to the lower sea of the rising sun [Persian Gulf]'.

Layard's discoveries proved Bible history to be correct. Shortly afterwards he found a Treasure Room full of the booty which had been taken from the captured cities of Judah. There were copper cauldrons, bronze bells, buttons and studs of ivory and pearl, lovely bowls of bronze, swords, daggers and shields, a throne of bronze with ivory feet. Many things just fell to pieces and dissolved into dust as soon as they were touched, but Layard was able to send many objects to the British Museum.

Henry Layard had heard of some gigantic rock carvings cut in a cliff face at Bavian, north east of Mosul. These had been described by an explorer named Ross, so Henry went to find them. On the high cliff north of the village were gigantic figures, the two chief ones picturing the same king, very like the builder of the palace of Nineveh. These two kings were making offerings to the gods. Inscriptions in cuneiform writing ran across the slabs. They were too high up for Henry to copy but he was determined to get them. He ordered his native servants to lower him on ropes from the top of the cliff till he reached a narrow ledge.

'Standing on a ledge scarcely six inches wide overlooking a giddy depth and in a constrained and painful position I had some difficulty in copying them', he wrote in his diary, but copy them he did, even at risk of his life. His servants hauled him clumsily up and down on the rope and all but dropped him to the bottom of the gorge. It was not till the inscriptions were deciphered two years later that he knew he had been looking at the great King Sennacherib's memorial. The inscription gave Sennacherib's name and titles and, even more interesting, an account of the great works undertaken by the king. It told how he had caused eighteen canals to be dug from the River Ussur and a canal from Kisri to Nineveh and 'brought waters through them'. This tremendous work of water-engineering made his lands fertile and provided water for his many flocks and herds. The inscription opened up yet another chapter in Assyrian history.

Layard went on a short tour with a tribe of friendly Arabs to explore the river Khabur in March and April 1850. 'Fat Toma' Shishman carried on with the digging while he was away. He discovered two chambers.

When Layard entered them he found the floors piled over a foot deep with baked clay tablets all inscribed with cuneiform writing. The tablets were of all sizes from nine inches square to small ones not more than an inch long. Layard had found the Royal Record Office and Library! He wrote to Canning, the British ambassador in Istanbul, 'They appear to be the records of some of the Nineveh kings. I have already six cases full and the room is not half emptied!'

There were *twenty-six thousand* of these inscribed clay tablets. Imagine Layard's joy and triumph when he uncovered them! These were some of the earliest writings in the world. He sent them to the British Museum for Rawlinson and Dr Hincks to decipher them.

They found the tablets dealt with many subjects: there were historical records of wars; laws made by the kings; letters between nations; lists of the gods and feast days. Five hundred tablets dealt with illnesses and gave prescriptions mentioning herbs to be used as drugs and physic. Other tablets gave instructions for making glass and glazes. There was a catalogue of the stars and a calendar, proving that the

Assyrians knew how to measure time and had some knowledge of mathematics. An account of the Flood was found, very like Noah's Flood in the Old Testament.

Perhaps these were the most valuable of all Layard's finds. He himself realized how valuable they were, for he wrote: 'We cannot overrate their value. They furnish us with materials for the complete deciphering of cuneiform writing, for restoring the language and history of Assyria and for enquiring into the customs, sciences and literature of its people. But years must elapse before the fragments can be put together and the inscriptions transcribed.'

The translation did take a very long time. The tablets, known as the Kuyunjik Collection, are in the British Museum

Tablets of medical texts from the library at Nineveh

in London and are still being studied to give information on the lives of the Assyrian people.

Layard spent the next few months packing up the treasures he had found and sending them to the British Museum. Then, ill with malaria and tired out, he set off for a holiday in the mountains of Kurdistan. He intended to look for unknown Assyrian ruins near the town and lake of Van. It was said that an Assyrian queen, Semiramis, had a summer palace there high in the hills, to escape the intense heat of Nineveh. There Layard found large inscriptions carved on the rock faces of the cliffs. He copied twenty-five of these. It was thirty-eight years later before these could be translated, for they were not like the other cuneiform writings he had found.

The party returned slowly through unexplored country to the south. Over a hundred miles away they saw the white-capped cone of Mount Ararat, the mountain upon which Noah's ark was said to have rested. They journeyed over terrifying rocky mountain passes, down narrow, cruel gorges where there was little foothold for horses, and down to the plain of the Tigris burning in the August sun.

Layard had decided to return to London. He was sick, weary, and out of patience with the meanness of the British Museum authorities. He had tried to do what was almost impossible on a very small grant. He wrote to the Prime Minister, Lord Palmerston, asking for leave to return home the following spring from his appointment at the British Embassy in Istanbul. Before he went, however, he decided to take a look at the abandoned ruins of the city of Babylon, much further down the Tigris.

His last task before leaving in mid-October 1850 was to see nearly a hundred cases of finds embarked on rafts to float down river to Baghdad. Layard went with the rafts, accompanied by Rassam and thirty of his best trained diggers.

The river Tigris wound sluggishly over a flat brown plain,

a waste of sandy wilderness over which the heat-waves danced. This was the ancient land of Sumeria known to the Old Testament writers as the Land of Shinar. Later it was named Babylonia. It was over this land that the flood poured when Noah built his ark. The great rivers Tigris and Euphrates then burst their banks and the muddy waters covered the plain. Layard, nearly 3,000 years later, spoke of the disgraceful neglect of the rivers. 'The Tigris and the Euphrates in the lower part of their course are breaking from their natural beds, forming vast marshes, turning fertile districts into a wilderness.'

As the rafts were carried along slowly by the sluggish currents he saw huge masses of ruined brick-work. 'These are the remains of the palaces and castles of the last Persian kings and of the first Caliphs.'

The low banks swarmed with Arabs living in their wretched mud hovels, their oxen trampling round and round as they turned water-wheels. It was a colourful scene: horse-men and riders on spirited steeds and white asses; Turks in flowing robes and large turbans; Persians in high black caps; Bedouins wearing striped cotton gowns, with red tasselled fezzes on their heads; ladies of Baghdad in scarlet and white draperies, their faces covered by black veils, with only their eyes showing above them.

Layard found Baghdad interesting. Its long covered bazaars sold goods from every land; spices, tea and porcelain from China; silks and silver-ware from Persia; leather from Turkey; dates from Arabia; furs from Russia; cotton materials and knives and guns from Britain. Baghdad was a link between the Far East and the West. For all the interest, Layard had a sense of disappointment. Gone were the palaces and gardens of Sultan Haroun-al-Rashid that Henry had dreamed over as a boy! Instead there were dirty, unsightly hovels.

D.O.L.T.—6

Layard and his team of diggers did not dare to venture very far afield, for the surrounding country was overrun by warlike Bedouins who pounced on the trading caravans and robbed them. Indeed, Layard's workmen did not dare to set up a camp near the ruins of Babylon, so Layard had to stay in the nearest town of Hillah where the Pasha or ruler promised him protection. From here each day Layard rode the few miles to Babylon.

There he investigated a great square mound called by the Arabs the Tower of Babel. He found many small objects like small clay figures near the surface. He dug some trenches into the great mound but he came on no wonderful sculptures. He found vast masses of brickwork but no inscribed clay tablets such as he had found at Nineveh. Babylon was just a huge heap of bricks, many, it is true, stamped with the name of Nebuchadnezzar and many glazed in bright colours. Layard wrote in disappointment to the British Museum that although small objects and inscriptions might be recovered, 'I question whether these would be worth the expense'. He reckoned it would cost £25,000 to dig out Babylon.

He was vexed that he could not even trace the walls of a single building: all were shapeless piles of masonry. The reason for this was that the palaces of Babylon had all been built of mud-dried bricks and these had crumbled with the passage of time. At Babylon there were no quarries of rock or alabaster. The only material to the builders' hands was mud-like *clay* which they mixed with chopped straw to bind it and then shape into bricks. Sometimes these were burned to make them hard; often they were just baked in the sun.

Many years later, between 1899 and 1914, a German, Doctor Koldewey, did manage to trace the walls of ancient Babylon. By then new ways of digging and new scientific methods to find the age and date of buildings had developed. Layard did the best he could with the small amount of money he was able to spend and the short time he had. It was amazing what he discovered at Nineveh and the furious rate he must have worked in the blazing sun to uncover all he did. Although this was not possible at Babylon, he had pointed the way for other diggers to follow. He had also located many other mounds in his travels. These proved in after years to be the ruins of other long-forgotten cities.

It was while Layard was searching the river swamps for these remains that he came on a great stretch of low sandy mounds. These were the ruins of the city of Nippur. Here he found a number of strange glazed coffins. Again, nearly a hundred years later, American archaeologists came to dig and found the remains of *twenty* cities built one on top of the other.

While he was searching for these ancient cities, Layard was taken seriously ill with pleurisy and fever. For two days he could not move from his bed. Reports came to him that bands of warlike Bedouins were approaching. There was danger that he and his men would be surrounded and cut off from Baghdad. Ill as he was he forced himself to mount his horse and ride for fourteen hours to Baghdad. As he passed through the city gates he collapsed. He was very ill but as soon as he recovered he was eager to travel again.

On the 27th February 1851 he left Baghdad and crossed the Tigris by a crazy bridge of boats.

'For some miles', he wrote, 'we watched the gilded domes and minarets rising above the dark belt of palms and glittering in the rays of the morning sun. At last they, too, vanished and I had looked for the last time on Baghdad.'

As he rode to Mosul he stopped on his way at Kalat Sherghat where he had left a party of workmen digging. They had not found much of importance but fifty years later a German team dug there till 1914 and found the oldest city, Ashur, the first capital of Assyria. Again Layard had pointed the way for other men to dig with success.

On they went towards Mosul. 'Our track led through a wilderness. We found no water nor saw any moving thing', he wrote. But there were moving things, evil things, stirring in the desert by night.

Layard wrote, 'I awoke in the middle of the night by an unusual noise close to my tent. I immediately gave the alarm but it was too late. Two of our horses had been stolen but in the darkness we could not pursue the thieves.'

They had travelled in the company of an Arab chief. He felt it was a slur on his honour that Layard's horses should have been stolen while they were under his protection. He vowed he would get the horses back again. He kept his word. He spent six weeks tracing them among the desert tribes, then brought them back to Layard at Mosul. He would take no reward. The honour of his tribe mattered more.

When Layard reached Kuyunjik again he found that Toma had opened four more chambers. The sculptured slab walls showed camels being loaded with spoil and the captives of Sennacherib's wars being tortured and killed. This was the last excavation that Layard undertook at Nineveh.

In his digging at Nineveh Layard had done almost impossible things. He had opened no less than seventy-one halls, chambers and passages, panelled in sculptured alabaster. These panels recorded the wars of great Assyrian kings. Layard had unearthed nearly *two miles* of these alabaster walls and found twenty-seven great doorways formed by tremendous winged bulls and lions. Besides all this he had drawn or taken impressions of the slabs he had not been able to move and had faithfully copied the inscriptions.

The most wonderful thing of all that he found was the great library of inscribed tablets. When these were deciphered, the history of Assyria and its people was revealed to the world. It was the beginning of the study of archaeology in

Layard copying bas reliefs at Kuyunjik (Nineveh)
From a drawing by S. C. Malan

the Near East, the cradle of civilization. Even Layard did not realize at the time what a tremendous thing he had achieved. It was now time for him to return to England.

'On the 28th April I bade a last farewell to my faithful Arab friends and with a heavy heart turned from the ruins of ancient Nineveh', Henry Layard wrote for the last time in his diary.

When he reached London in July 1851 he found himself a famous man. His book, *Nineveh and Its Remains* had proved a popular success. At the great Crystal Palace Exhibition in London in 1851 people thronged in thousands to see 'Nineveh Court', copied from what Layard had described of the palaces at Kuyunjik and Khorsabad, with two actual alabaster bulls from Khorsabad. This exhibition and his book made Henry a hero in the public eye. But praise from the English people was not enough to keep him. He was hard put to it to know what to do next to support himself. He wrote to a friend, 'I have no means of making ends meet without some employment'.

He set to work to write another book, *Discoveries in the Ruins of Nineveh and Babylon*, but the writing took some time. It was 1853 before the book was published, but by July that year over 12,000 copies had been sold. He also published a book of engravings, *A Second Series of the Monuments of Nineveh*. These two books gave him a little time to consider what he would do next, but he knew he must soon find some new work to do.

'I should like to get into Parliament in England. I think that, once there, I could push my way', he wrote to a friend. Layard was always ambitious.

In February 1852, to his own surprise, he was offered a post as Under Secretary of State for Foreign Affairs, an appointment in the Civil Service. He was delighted, for he had always hoped for such a post. He filled it for several

months, then in July 1852 there came a Parliamentary General
Election. Henry decided to try his luck as the Liberal
Candidate for Aylesbury. He was successfully elected and
cheering crowds followed him in a triumphal procession
through Aylesbury with flag waving and flower throwing.
For five years Henry Layard was Member of Parliament for
Aylesbury.

In the spring of 1853 there was trouble between Russia
and Turkey. Layard was sent to Constantinople to see how
matters stood. When he returned to England he warned the
Government how serious the situation was. The following
year, 1854, war was declared against Russia, and Britain
became the ally of Turkey. British and Turkish troops landed
on the Crimean peninsula on the Black Sea. The Crimean
War had begun.

The British went into the war ill prepared. The army was
badly provisioned with food and badly clothed to face the
bitter winter of the Crimea. A British resident at Constantinople reported, 'Our men are dying of famine and exposure
at a fearful rate; all might have been averted by the simplest
forethought and care'.

Henry Layard was very angry at the stupid way the war
was being conducted, and so was Charles Dickens with whom
Henry had become friends in 1853. They organized a meeting
at the Drury Lane Theatre to protest against the way the
Government was handling the war. This made a lot of
enemies for Layard among the Government. In March 1857
he was defeated at the General Election and ceased for a time
to be a Member of Parliament. He was, however, elected in
1859 as the Member of Parliament for Southwark. Once
again he was given the post of Under Secretary for Foreign
Affairs.

In 1869 Henry Layard married Enid Guest, the daughter
of his cousin Lady Charlotte Guest. She was a beautiful young

woman, tall and stately. She was twenty-seven years younger
than Henry, but for all that theirs was a very happy marriage
and she proved a great helpmate to him. Layard was then
fifty-two years old.

After he was married he revived his old interest in Italian
art. Just as he had done when he was a child and a young
man, he now spent a holiday each year in Italy and began to
write about Italian painters.

In 1880 one of his youthful dreams came true. He was
appointed Ambassador to Turkey. Once more he returned
to Constantinople. It was not as a penniless man that he
returned this time, however, Before he left Britain Queen
Victoria knighted him and he was now Sir Henry Layard.
Not only that; the Queen lent her own royal yacht, the
Osborne, to take him and his beautiful wife from Brindisi in
Italy to Constantinople. One can imagine Henry's feelings as
the magnificent yacht passed through the Sea of Marmora
and anchored in the Golden Horn and he looked up at the
hill of Pera and the British Embassy. He must have thought
of his first arrival in Turkey just over forty years earlier when
he came as a poor young man on horseback. At that time he
collapsed with fever and came close to death. This arrival was
so different. THEN he 'did not know where to look for a
dinner'; NOW he was received with great honour and a
banquet was arranged.

The Turks looked on him as a friend. He understood them
well, knew and respected their customs; spoke their language.
For over a year he held the position of Ambassador, well
loved by all the people. Then he returned to Italy with his
wife. They lived for many years in Venice, coming often to
stay in their English home.

Austen Henry Layard died in London on 5th July 1894
at the age of seventy-seven, mourned by all who admired
his great work in Assyria. The wonderful sculptured and

carved alabaster slabs in the British Museum are his memorial. He had covered again with earth most of the palaces he had found, to preserve them. One can imagine him shaking his head as he wrote, 'We look in vain for any traces of the wonderful remains we have just seen and are half inclined to believe that we have dreamed a dream or have been listening to some tale of eastern romance'.

It was a tale 'of eastern romance' that led him in the first place to Nineveh. It began with a small boy lying under a dining-room table so that he might get peace to read *The Arabian Nights*.

He finished his book on Nineveh and Babylon by writing: 'Some, who may hereafter tread on the spot when the grass again grows over the ruins of the Assyrian palaces, may indeed suspect I have been relating a vision.'

It was a vision that led other archaeologists to dig where he had dug. There they are still finding priceless treasures of the past.

Walter Savage Landor, the poet who had known Layard when he was a child, wrote this of him,

> My song shall rise
> Although none heed or hear it; rise it shall,
> And swell along the wastes of Nineveh
> And Babylon, until it reach to thee,
> Layard, who raisest cities from the dust.

Austen Henry Layard reopened a great chapter of the world's history for us. Because of him, Nineveh and Babylon were indeed raised from the dust.

○○

PART TWO

HENRY SCHLIEMANN

Henry Schliemann
1822–90

CHAPTER ONE

○○○

Poverty and Shipwreck

A small boy pored over the book his father had given him for Christmas. It showed a burning city and a warrior in armour carrying out an old man on his back.

'There must be something of the old city of Troy left,' the boy declared. 'Look, Father, you can see the walls still standing among the flames.'

'That's just a fanciful picture. All the city of Troy was burned to the ground,' his father told him.

'Where is Troy? Please tell me about it,' Henry Schliemann asked his father.

'It was a city far away on the shores of Asia Minor. The King of Troy was Priam and he had a son called Paris. Paris stole away the wife of the King of Sparta. She was Helen, the most beautiful woman in the world.'

'That was a wrong thing to do,' Henry said gravely.

'Yes, it was. He took her to Troy and the King of Sparta and his brother Agamemnon, another king of Mycenae, went to fetch her back. That started a war between the Greeks and the Trojans that lasted ten years.'

'And what happened in the end?'

'After a long siege the Greeks managed to get into the city

by a trick. They pretended to withdraw their army as if they were going away. They left a large wooden horse outside the gates of Troy. The Trojans thought it was an offering to the gods and dragged it inside the gates. Inside the horse were concealed a number of Greek soldiers. When the Trojans slept they emerged, overcame the guard at the city gates and

Homer: inspirer of Henry's daydreams

opened the gates and let in a large number of the Greek army who were waiting hidden near by. Troy was taken in terrible fighting and much of it was burned to the ground. Homer tells us this story.'

'Who is Homer?' Henry asked.

'He was a famous Greek poet who wrote about the siege of Troy in a book called the *Iliad*. Probably a lot of his story is just fanciful.'

'I think it could be *true*,' Henry declared. He looked again at the picture in his book. 'Those big walls couldn't be destroyed altogether. I'm sure some of them must be there still.'

His father smiled. 'Think that if you like, my boy, but I am sure nothing remains of Troy today.'

'Some day I shall go and see for myself,' Henry said obstinately. 'Some day I shall find the walls of Troy and under the ruins there will be treasure of gold. I shall go and dig it out.'

'You are just a dreamer,' his father laughed. 'You are always making up stories of buried treasure.'

Henry had a great friend, Minna the daughter of a neighbouring farmer. Together the two of them roamed the old castle of Ankershagen in Germany where they lived. Henry, whose German name was Heinrich, was the son of the minister in the church at Ankershagen. He was one of a large family. Minna and he were eight years old. Minna believed in all Henry's dreams and she was his constant companion in adventures to try to find buried treasure. Always they kept dreaming and talking about Troy. Then, two years later, the dream suddenly came to an end.

Two things happened to turn Henry's world upside down. First his mother died; then immediately afterwards Henry's father fell into disgrace. For some time there had been murmurings against him by the people of his parish. Now it was whispered that he was taking the church funds and using them for his own purposes. No one would have anything to do with him. The disgrace even fell upon his children, too. Minna's parents forbade her to go any more to the Schliemanns' house and her friendship with Henry came to an end. He was broken-hearted without her companionship. He crept about the house miserably till even his father noticed his unhappiness. He decided to send his children away from Ankershagen till the trouble blew over. Henry was sent to stay with his uncle who was the minister at Kalkhorst.

His Uncle Frederick was a kind man who saw that Henry was an intelligent boy. He began to instruct the lad in Latin and sent him to school. There Henry worked very hard and his teacher advised his uncle that he should go to a more advanced school. The fees at this school were rather high but Henry's father managed to spare the money for a time.

Henry liked his new school and was looking forward to learning Greek when yet another blow fell. The church authorities would not allow his father to be a minister any longer and he had to leave his house which belonged to the church. He could no longer afford to pay Henry's school fees and Henry had to go back to his former school, which was free, and there was no one there to teach him Greek. In spite of his disappointment Henry worked hard at school for the next three years. Then he received another letter from his father.

'I can no longer even afford the money necessary for your keep while you attend school. You must go out into the world and earn your own living, for I cannot continue to support you.'

Henry's uncle could not afford to keep him either. Henry would have to find a job, any job that would give him food and lodging. Henry was bewildered, not knowing where to turn.

'Perhaps a shop? A grocer's shop, for at least there would be food there to eat,' he told himself.

He went to see Mr Holst, a grocer in the neighbouring town of Furstenburg.

'Yes, I could do with a lad to help in the shop. Are you a good riser?' Mr Holst asked. 'You would have to be up at five o'clock to sweep and dust before the shop is opened.'

Henry was a little taken aback, but he said, 'Yes, I can get up early.'

'Right, then. I will take you on. All your food found and you will have a bed under the counter.'

In those days shop assistants slept on the premises in small shops and had a mattress under the counter for a bed.

'And . . . and the wages?' Henry stammered.

'Wages! Many a lad would be glad to work for his keep.'

'I . . . I must have some wages. I shall have clothes to buy,' Henry insisted.

'Very well, then. I will give you twenty talers at the end of the year, but not till then,' Mr Holst agreed in a grudging voice.

A taler was worth about five shillings, so Henry's wages would be less than two shillings a week! There seemed to be no other job open to him, so Henry agreed to start work in the shop.

For the next five years Henry Schliemann lived a life of utter drudgery. He rose at dawn, dusted, swept, cleaned Mr Holst's boots and laid out the goods on the counter before he had his own miserable breakfast. He carried sacks of potatoes to the distillery to be made into the potato whiskey that Mr Holst sold. He trundled heavy casks round the shop. All day he stood behind the counter selling butter, milk, coffee, candles, oil till eleven o'clock at night when the shop shut. Only then, tired out, was he free to roll on to his hard bed under the counter. Most of all he was miserable because he had no chance of continuing his studies. His master would not let him burn candles at night and the shop was always dark and cold. The only chance he got to read his precious books was in the early summer mornings and on Sundays when the shop was closed. His life seemed to be spent between the counter and the shop door. All the will to learn seemed to be crushed out of him. Then, one day, a kind of miracle happened.

A tipsy miller came into the shop to buy whiskey. He was a young man who had had a good education but who had come down in the world due to his foolish drinking. He sat down on the counter and began to recite lines in Greek from the poet Homer's *Iliad*. Henry listened entranced to the lovely music of the words, though he did not understand them.

'Say it again! Say it again, please!' he begged.

The good-natured miller obliged, but Henry was not satisfied till he had heard it a third time and the miller tried to translate it.

'Some day I *will* learn Greek,' Henry vowed.

From then on he dreamed of escape from the slavery of the grocer's shop. He thought of going to America. Many young Germans were emigrating to America at that time and tales came to Germany of the fortunes they were making. Henry wrote to his father to borrow the money to pay his fare to America, promising to pay it back as soon as he could. His father was not able to lend him the money.

'Shall I have to serve behind this counter for the rest of my life?' Henry asked himself bitterly.

Though it seemed very unlucky at the time, an accident happened to him which changed the course of his whole life. The grocer asked Henry to lift a case of chicory from one side of the shop to the other. It was not a big one but it was very heavy. The strain of lifting it was too much. He burst a blood-vessel in his chest and the blood gushed from his mouth. From that moment Henry knew he could no longer go on lifting sacks of potatoes and casks of whiskey. The same thing might happen again. He had to lie on his bed for a few days till he was healed, and during that time he decided, 'I will go to Hamburg. From there I might get a ship to America if I can scrape the fare together.'

He had managed to save in German money what would be equal to about £7 out of his miserable wages during the past years. This money and the clothes he stood up in were all he possessed. He set out to walk to Hamburg. On the way, as he walked, he taught himself book-keeping from a book he carried in his pocket.

Henry was fascinated by the towers and spires of Hamburg and the princely houses of the merchants. He wandered down to the docks and looked at the great ships bound for America. First, though, he must find a job and save money. He turned to the only work he knew, a grocer's assistant. He did not last long at it, only eight days! No one wanted a youth who was not strong enough to lift heavy cases and sacks. In despair, seeing his small store of money dwindling away, Henry wrote to another uncle for a small loan to help him till he found a job. His uncle lent it to him, but with the money he sent a mean, unkind letter.

Hamburg: fascinating to the young Henry Schliemann

Henry would have sent the money back to him at once, but he was near starvation and hunger makes one swallow pride. He determined to repay his uncle as soon as he could scrape the money together. Later in his life he did indeed repay it.

Once again when things seemed desperate Henry had a stroke of luck. He met a man who had been brought up alongside his mother in childhood. Mr Wendt was surprised to see the son of his old playmate Louise. 'What are you doing in Hamburg?' he asked Henry.

'Trying to earn money to get to America,' Henry told him.

Mr Wendt thought hard for a minute or two. 'How would you like to go to *South* America? Can you speak Spanish?'

'No, but I could learn sufficient on the voyage there,' Henry replied with confidence. He was quick at learning languages.

'Then I could get you a post at La Guayra. The brig *Dorothea* is sailing shortly for South America. I will ask the captain to let you have a cheap passage. He is a friend of mine.'

So it was settled that Henry Schliemann should seek his fortune in South America. He sold his silver watch to buy himself a blanket, two shirts, a coat and an extra pair of trousers, and also a Spanish grammar. With this outfit he set sail from Hamburg in November 1841. He was nineteen years old.

The *Dorothea* carried a crew of eighteen men and three passengers. Henry was very sea-sick and this grew worse when the ship reached the North Sea. A hurricane blew and waves broke right over the ship. She sprang a leak and the pumps had to be kept going night and day.

'Here, lad! Try chewing some ship's biscuits quite dry. It's better than being sea-sick on an empty stomach,' the first mate advised Henry. Curiously, he did feel better after eating the dry biscuits. He roped himself to his bunk to keep from falling out when the ship rolled; then pulled out his Spanish grammar and set to work to prepare himself for his new life in South America.

The storm grew worse. Snow fell and the ship hurtled like a shuttle-cock from the crests of mountainous waves to the troughs below. There was a joiner among the passengers who had horrible forebodings of disaster. So had his son. 'Did you hear the ship's cat whining all night and the captain's dog howling?' the joiner's son asked. '*They* know something terrible is going to happen.'

Even the cabin boy was full of fears when he brought them tea and biscuits. 'Let's hope we're all alive to have tea tomorrow morning,' he said gloomily.

Henry climbed into his bunk and tried to sleep. At midnight the cabin door flew open. The captain put in his head, shouting, 'All passengers on deck! The ship is going down!' Hard on his words a huge wave stove in the port-hole sending a flood of water into the cabin.

The passengers sprang out of their bunks and rushed on deck. There was no time even to dress. Henry was wearing only a pair of woollen drawers. He snatched up his blanket but when he reached the deck he had to drop it and cling to the rail. Another wave burst over the ship and swept him to the starboard side where he managed to grab a rope and hang on. He felt desperately afraid. For half an hour he and his companions clung to the rope. The joiner prayed aloud. All the time, as the ship tossed, the ship's bell rang like a death knell.

The *Dorothea* took a terrible battering and sank lower and lower in the water. The sky was black and the snow swirled round them. Chilled to the bone, half naked, Henry still hung on to his rope.

'Climb into the rigging, lads! You're less likely to be washed overboard,' the first mate shouted.

Henry let go his rope to follow the seaman. Just then a huge wave caught the ship broadside on. With a horrific crash the brig heeled over the port side, failed to right herself and sank, taking Henry Schliemann down with her.

With his lungs almost bursting for breath Henry fought his way to the surface again. A dark object floated by him. It was an empty cask. Henry grabbed at it and fastened his grip on the rim. Now tossed on the crest of a wave, now wallowing in the depths of a trough, he went up and down like a cork through the darkness of the night. When dawn came he saw a boat close by. Henry shouted with all the strength that remained to him.

It was the stern boat of the *Dorothea* which had been thrown clear of the ship. In it were the first mate and thirteen other people who had managed to scramble on board. They had no oars and only a plank of wood with which to paddle a boat.

'Try to swim to us!' the first mate shouted to Henry.

Henry kicked out but kept his hold on the cask. Somehow, using the wooden plank, the first mate managed to turn the boat towards him. Yard by yard the boat came nearer, then the first mate leaned out and grabbed Henry by the hair. With a superhuman effort he got Henry under the arms and managed to drag him over the stern and into the boat. Shivering, Henry cowered for warmth among the other folk.

They drifted till morning, then the tide threw up the boat on a sand-bank off the island of Texel on the Dutch coast. The storm was dying down and the fisher-folk of Texel came hurrying to gather up the cargo that was drifting ashore from the wreck.

They found the survivors lying gasping on the sand-bank. Henry Schliemann was in very bad shape with cuts on his face and body, three front teeth broken and badly swollen feet. A farmer came along with his cart and carried them to the farm-house. There they warmed themselves by the fire and drank coffee.

'Poor chap! We'll have to find some clothes for you. It's a wonder you haven't perished of cold,' the farmer told Henry. 'Here's a pair of trousers. Put this old blanket round you for a coat. You'll have to wear a pair of Dutch clogs on your feet.'

Once again, though, Henry's luck held good. Among the cargo that was washed ashore was his sea-chest. In it were his shirts and stockings and his pocket book with a small amount of money. He was the only one to be so lucky.

The German Consul offered to send the survivors back to Germany. 'What about you?' he asked Henry.

'No, thank you. I was not happy in Germany. If the good God cast me ashore in Holland, may be he meant me to stay here,' Henry decided. 'I will go to Amsterdam.'

In Amsterdam he got a bed at a lodging house for sailors, but his funds were low and he was very weak and ill. He asked the Consul for help, who sent him to hospital.

While there Henry wrote to his friend, Mr Wendt, the merchant of Hamburg who had sent him on his voyage. He told him all about the shipwreck and what had befallen him. By a lucky chance his letter arrived when Mr Wendt was entertaining other merchants to dinner. Mr Wendt thought his letter very interesting and read it aloud to his friends. They all thought Henry deserved pity and help. One guest suggested a whip-round among the wealthy merchants and the result was a collection of 240 gulden in German money, worth about £25 in English money. It seemed a small fortune to Henry who had never had so much money in all his life. With the money came a letter of introduction to the

Prussian consul, asking him to find work for the young
man.

In a few days a job was found for Henry as a messenger
in the counting house of T. C. Quien at a wage equal to
about a pound a week. Out of this he had to pay for a bare
uncomfortable room in a lodging house and to buy his food,
which had to be of the plainest. The only money he spent
was on books to try to continue his education. He saw this
as the only way to get on in the world.

Every moment he could spare from his work was given up
to learning languages. First he tackled English. He bought an
English grammar and two books, *The Vicar of Wakefield* and
Ivanhoe, and he read them over and over again till he knew
them almost by heart. Every Sunday he went twice to the
English church in Amsterdam so that he could listen to the
minister preaching. In six months he could speak and write
English fluently. The next six months he spent learning
French. To these languages he added Spanish, Italian and
Portuguese. He had a wonderful memory and a gift for
learning languages. In just over two years he learned six
languages and was able to speak and understand them well.

When he was twenty-two he decided to look for a post
where he could use these languages. He applied for a situation
with Schroeders, a big trading firm in Amsterdam. Mr
Schroeder himself interviewed him.

'What are your qualifications?' he asked Henry.

'I can speak and read seven languages easily and I can do
book-keeping. Mr Quien will vouch for my honesty. I have
worked for him for over two years.'

Mr Schroeder engaged him and Schliemann became a
book-keeper in his counting house. There he worked very
hard and pleased Mr Schroeder who began to give him
foreign letters to translate.

'Here's a letter from Russia. I suppose you don't know

Russian too, Henry?' Mr Schroeder teased him gently. He had a high regard for his young clerk's ability.

'Give me a few weeks and I will know Russian too,' Henry replied promptly.

He worked every spare minute at learning Russian, even thinking in this new language. At the end of six weeks he was able to write his first letter in Russian.

Schroeders did a big trade with Russia in indigo, a blue dye that was made from the indigo plant. This dye was used by cloth-makers all over the world. Henry was chosen to talk to the Russian traders who came to Amsterdam. Mr Schroeder watched him with interest. In December 1845 he called Schliemann into his office.

'Henry, how would you like to go to St Petersburg as our representative there?' he asked.

Amsterdam: here Henry began to prosper

St Petersburg was the old name for Leningrad and it was then the principal trading city in Russia.

Henry did not reply for a minute, but turned the matter over in his mind. 'Would you allow me to do a little trading on my own account, too?' he asked.

Mr Schroeder thought hard for a minute or two also. He had always found Henry perfectly honest. 'So long as you do not permit it to interfere with our business,' he agreed.

Henry set off in the depths of winter by coach and sleigh for St Petersburg to represent one of the most famous trading firms in the world. He had come a very long way in a few years from being a penniless, shipwrecked youth.

CHAPTER TWO

○○○

American Gold Rush

Henry Schliemann prospered well in St Petersburg. While there he also took several journeys abroad for Schroeders. He visited Britain and spent a whole Sunday in the British Museum looking at Egyptian mummies and Greek and Roman vases. Here perhaps he found once more the interest in Greek antiquities that was later to shape his whole life. He visited Manchester too and was amazed at the many factories built there and the great ironworks where locomotives for the new railways were being built.

Back in Russia he made a small fortune in the indigo trade and he now thought he could afford to get married. He thought of Minna, his childhood's playmate. He had always dreamed of marrying her one day when he had enough money, but he had never told her this. Now he wrote to her parents asking for her hand in marriage. In 1846 this was the correct way that young people went about marriage, first to obtain the parents' consent. To his dismay he received a letter to tell him that only a few weeks earlier Minna had married a farmer. Henry was bitterly disappointed and quite cast down. For a time he thought of nothing but making money and yet more money.

He might have gone on piling up a fortune in Russia, but in 1850 he got another shock which stung him into action. His brother Ludwig died suddenly in California. At that time California was in the middle of a gold rush. Gold had been discovered in the Sacramento Valley. Miners and adventurers from all over the world dashed to California to dig for it. Ludwig had made a fortune as a kind of banker, dealing in gold with the diggers. Henry decided he must go to Sacramento and find out what had become of the fortune Ludwig had written to say he had made. On 28th December 1850 he sailed for New York in the *S.S. Atlantic* from Liverpool.

Eight days out from Liverpool the ship struck a heavy storm. A huge wave smashed the port paddle-wheel and the main shaft broke. These were the early days of steam-ships when they also carried sails in case the engine broke down. The ship was in mid-Atlantic, 1,800 miles from Liverpool. The captain hoisted his sails and tried to make headway against a fierce westerly gale.

'The sails look like handkerchiefs', Henry wrote in his diary. He was badly sea-sick again.

The rest of the passengers were terrified what might happen if the sails were ripped to pieces. They begged the captain to turn about and run before the wind and make for Britain again. In the end this was what he was forced to so. Sixteen days later the passengers were set ashore in southern Ireland.

Henry was not in the least daunted by his second escape from possible shipwreck. At once he went to Liverpool and took the very next ship for New York.

From New York he took a ship to the Isthmus of Panama, the narrow neck of land that joins North America to South America. Today the Panama Canal is cut through it and great ships can sail from the Atlantic to the Pacific Ocean. In 1850 there was no canal there and people who wanted to get from

Colon on the Atlantic to Panama on the Pacific Ocean had to journey on mules through the jungle. They went in armed parties because of bandits. Henry carried his money in a belt round his waist under his clothes and he was armed with a revolver and a dagger.

'It is a fantastic country', he wrote in his diary. 'I have seen alligators in the Chagres River and butterflies as big as pigeons.'

From Panama he sailed for California. It was a horrible voyage. The weather was hot and steamy and the food was awful. Salt pork or corned beef was served up at every meal. Henry hated the sea-trip but at last he reached San Francisco. He went straight to Sacramento to look after his brother Ludwig's affairs. He discovered that Ludwig's partner had vanished and taken Ludwig's fortune with him!

'There is nothing I can do about it,' Henry told himself. 'But if Ludwig could make a fortune here, then so can I! It is always the man who buys and sells the gold who makes the most money in the end. I'll set up as a buyer of gold dust, buying from the miners and selling to the big banks in San Francisco.'

Sacramento, a place to sell gold dust

Before he began business, he visited the banking firm of Rothschild in San Francisco to make arrangements with them. While he was there, he nearly lost his life once more, this time not by drowning but by fire.

Henry was staying at the Union Hotel near the centre of the city. He had had a tiring day so he went to bed early. Hardly had he fallen asleep than he was wakened by the clanging of a bell, shouts in the street below and the sound of many running feet. He popped his head out of the bedroom door. There was a man running along the passage, his clothes in his arms.

'What's going on?' Henry cried.

'Fire! Fire!' the man shouted over his shoulder.

'Is the hotel on fire?'

'No, but it soon will be!' The man vanished round the turn of the stairs.

Henry dashed back to his room and flung on his clothes. He made sure he had his money belt and he stuffed other papers into his pockets. There was no time to pack his bag. Already the red light of the flames seemed to be dancing round the hotel. He fled down the stairs and into the smoke-filled street. A strong wind was blowing the sparks and flames towards the hotel. Henry stopped, bewildered, not knowing which way to run. A man gripped him by the arm. He was another of the hotel guests.

'Quick! Up to Telegraph Hill behind the town. The flames cannot reach us there.'

'Which way?' Henry panted, running alongside him.

'Follow me!'

Breathless and coughing with the smoke they reached Telegraph Hill where most of the people of San Francisco stood watching their city burn.

The wind had grown to almost a hurricane. It fanned the flames to a roar. The very ground in the streets seemed to have taken fire. This was because many of the roads were made of wooden planks placed over hollows and ditches. These acted like great blow-pipes through which the flames rushed, burning the planks. Showers of sparks were blown across the streets, setting fire to the wooden roofs of the timber houses on the other side. Most of the houses were built of wood but there were some brick ones with iron shutters and doors. Some folk thought they would be safe inside these but in the intense heat the bricks began to crumble and the metal doors to buckle. People who tried to get out of them found that the doors had jammed with the heat. They were prisoners in furnaces in which they roasted alive. Their terrible shrieks added to the din which rose from the burning city.

Firemen did their best to fight the flames and directed the water from their hoses at the very heart of the fire. The heat was so great that even the jets of water turned to steam. The roar of an explosion shook Telegraph Hill.

'What's that?' Henry gasped.

'It could be a store of gunpowder blowing up,' his companion told him. 'Plenty of gunpowder in the city! They'll be blowing up houses, too, so as to make a gap in the path of the flames.'

Another roar and the noise of falling walls proved the truth of what he said. Even these desperate measures failed to stop the fire spreading.

'There's not enough water in the city to fight the flames,' the man told Henry. 'There's always a shortage in summer and the houses are dry as tinder.'

Henry sniffed at the air. 'What's that I can smell? Vinegar?'

'Aye. Drewitt's are using the store of vinegar in their warehouse to save their premises. There's no water for the hoses so they are using their eighty thousand gallons of vinegar to stop the fire burning their warehouse.'

Great tongues of flame leaped from a thousand burning houses. The light from them fell over Telegraph Hill as strong as sunlight.

'How did the fire start?' Henry asked.

'In a paint shop near the hotel. Some folk think it was started by fire-raisers to destroy the city.'

'Surely not?' Henry was quite shocked.

'Yes, indeed. In a big fire like this folk run out of their homes and they forget to lock the doors. There are plenty of pickings for lawless thieves. This is the fourth big fire in San Francisco. If the folk of San Francisco catch them looting they'll tear them to bits.'

Indeed, there were many bad characters attracted by the gold in California. Henry found this out when he set up his gold-dust-buying business in Sacramento. For months he conducted business with a couple of pistols handy in his belt. He even slept beside his safe where the gold was stored. Though the door was bolted and the windows shuttered and barred, he hardly dared to sleep. In a letter to a friend he wrote, 'Never a negro slave works harder than I do. But it is nothing to the dangers of sleeping the night alone with immense amounts of gold. I spend the night in a feverish horror with loaded pistols in both hands. The noise of a mouse or a rat strikes me with terror.'

After Henry had caught the yellow fever three times, he decided he had had enough of California. He arranged with Rothschilds to transfer his money to Russia and he set off on the long journey home again. At Panama he joined a party going on mules through the jungle to Colon on the Atlantic coast.

Henry was not so lucky this time. This was the worst season of the year to journey through tropical jungle. The rain fell unceasingly in drenching torrents. The heat made the forests steam. The jungle trail was deep in mud. Halfway

San Francisco destroyed by fire
From a drawing in the Illustrated London News, *19 July 1851*

across the isthmus the Indian guides refused to go any further. They made off and with them they took all the food and water. The abandoned travellers were in despair and wondered whether to turn back.

Henry pointed out that it was as far to go back as to go on. 'We shall only have to make the journey again if we want to get to Colon. Let us push on. The trail is fairly well-marked.'

They plodded on through the dense green jungle. Rattle-snakes darted across their path and some of the men were stung by scorpions. For food they shot monkeys and ate them; they caught lizards too, skinned them and ate the flesh raw. They had no maps and only a compass to guide them. Some fell by the trail exhausted. They had to be left to die where they fell. When they made camp at night Henry fastened the bag containing his papers and valuables to his belt. He slept uneasily with his pistol in his hand.

'I will get through and take my possessions with me,' he vowed through clenched teeth.

Once he stumbled and fell. He looked up to see two men standing over him waiting to see if he would rise. They were ready to grab his pistol and money if he did not. He struggled to his feet, pistol in hand and glared at them and they slipped away. In the fall he had gashed his ankle and he found it hard to hobble and keep up with the others. The ankle began to fester.

At last the survivors struggled in to Colon, mere skeletons of themselves, dirty, their clothing in tatters. Henry wrote about the journey. 'Even now at a later date I cannot think about it without cold and trembling horror.' It was so terrible that he never spoke of it again.

Colon in Panama
From the Illustrated London News, *21 July 1888*

Once more he returned to Russia and became a very prosperous merchant indeed. He married Catherine Lyschin, a beautiful Russian, but the marriage proved a mistake. She had a terrible temper and made his life a misery and told him she had only married him for his money. Henry took refuge in his business, working twelve to fourteen hours a day, but it seemed the richer he became, the less use his money was to him.

He had never forgotten the drunken miller reciting Homer's poetry and the promise he had made himself that one day he would learn Greek. Now he could afford to do so. On Sundays he shut himself in his study with a teacher of Greek and worked at the language with great concentration. Its beauty and music uplifted him.

'Now I can read Homer's poems in his own tongue', he wrote with delight. 'There is no other language so noble. I must go to Greece.'

His teacher was a Greek priest, Theokletos Vimpos, who was a man of deep understanding and sympathy. A strong friendship grew between them, a friendship that was to have a great influence on Henry's later life, though he did not know it then.

Henry decided to leave his business and to try to seek peace of mind by travelling in distant lands. He begged his wife to go with him too, but she would not. She stayed in Russia and Henry made her a generous allowance of money.

Henry wandered through Egypt, India, Java, China, Japan, but still he did not go to Greece. He was immensely interested in the Great Wall of China. Old cities were beginning to mean a very great deal to him, even more than his prosperous business. The thought of the burnt walls of Troy was still at the back of his mind. He came back home and wrote an account of his journeys in French.

At last in the spring of 1866 he decided to sell his business and go to Paris and attend the University there. For several years he lived in Paris, attending lectures and studying. Henry Schliemann the merchant became Henry Schliemann the scholar. Catherine refused to join him, though he bought a beautiful house for her. Henry was bitterly unhappy. He did not know what to do with his life. So much wealth and he did not know how to spend it! Then, with a strange comfort, he thought of Homer and Greece.

'I will go to Greece,' he decided. 'I will find out if there is *truth* in Homer's stories, as I have always believed there was. I will go and dig in Greece to find the old cities that Homer writes about in his great poems, the *Iliad* and the *Odyssey*.'

Henry went to Ithaca, an island off the west coast of Greece that had been the home of Odysseus, Homer's Greek hero. From the moment he set foot on Ithaca Henry was like a new man.

'Every hill, stone, stream and olive grove spoke to me of Homer,' he declared. He met a miller with a donkey who was willing to take him exploring the island. What was more the miller knew all the legends of Odysseus and enjoyed telling them to Schliemann. Henry read the Odyssey and decided that Homer had described the palace of Odysseus on the top of Mount Aetos. There were the remains of ruined walls there which seemed to give colour to the story. Henry made up his mind to start digging in that place.

At five o'clock in the morning he climbed to the peak with four labourers. They commenced digging at the north-east corner inside the wall. After several hours' work they had found nothing, so Henry moved them to another place. After three hours' digging they reached the foundation stones of a small building. Then Henry himself found a semi-circular stone covered by earth. He thought it was a small altar and he lifted it. Four inches below it his pick-axe shattered a beautiful little vase. Henry was dismayed when he broke it, but he went on digging, moving the earth a little at a time, very carefully, and before long he found twenty more vases like it, beautifully made.

Henry accomplished his first digging: he had made his first discovery of the treasures of the past. This was just the beginning but it had kindled a spark in him. From now on he knew exactly what he wanted to do.

'Homer has led me aright. I will trust Homer and prove that what he has written about Troy is true too,' Henry said.

The Isle of Ithaca

CHAPTER THREE

○○○

Discoveries at Troy

H enry Schliemann went first to Athens to see his old friend Theokletos Vimpos, who was now a bishop. They met with great joy and Henry told Vimpos of his plan to go to Troy and dig there to find the old city. Then Henry left Athens and journeyed by way of Constantinople (Istanbul) and across the Sea of Marmora to the windy plain where Troy was supposed to be. The dream of his childhood was about to come true. First, though, he had to decide exactly where Troy might lie buried and where he was to dig.

Many people thought that Bunabashi, a village ten miles from the sea, was the site of ancient Troy. There was another place, the hill of Hissarlik, at the end of the valley near the sea, that other people thought might have been Troy. Whenever Henry was in doubt he read what Homer had to say about it. Always he carried a copy of the *Iliad* in his pocket.

He flicked the pages over. 'Whenever Homer speaks of the fighting between the Achaeans and the Trojans, he mentions that the Achaeans were near to their ships. Ah, yes, here's the place. "The Achaeans made seven or eight journeys a day from their ships to the city of Troy." That's plain enough. If Troy was at Bunabashi they'd have to journey over *seventy* miles each day. That's impossible! But if Troy was on the hill of Hissarlik, that's less than three miles away. They could make seven trips a day from their fleet easily enough then. The old city *must* be under the hill of Hissarlik. I shall dig there for Troy.'

An Englishman, Frank Calvert, owned half the hill of Hissarlik. Calvert agreed with Schliemann that this hill was the site of ancient Troy. He had already done some digging there but he had made no discoveries. He and Henry became friends and Calvert was quite willing to let him dig in his part of the hill. Henry talked to Calvert about his ideas of where he should dig.

'I am sure that Troy and the ruins of King Priam's palace lie near the top of the hill. If we lift off the top crust of earth we shall come on the marble palaces, the great gates and towers and perhaps even the buried treasure of King Priam. Who knows? I shall start digging at the top of the hill.'

'Perhaps you are right, Schliemann.' Calvert smiled kindly at Henry's enthusiasm. 'That part of the hill, though, does *not* belong to me. Before you could dig there you would have to get permission from the Turkish government. There would have to be preparations for the digging, too; the buying of spades and pickaxes and wheelbarrows and you would need a gang of trustworthy labourers. By the time you have done all that, it will be too late in the season to start digging, for the rains and bad weather will be upon us. It would be better to make a start on the digging next spring when you have all these matters arranged.'

Henry looked decidedly dashed.

'Come, man, the hill will not run away,' Calvert laughed.

Schliemann saw the wisdom of Calvert's advice. He agreed it was better to make preparations first. He also had to pay a visit to America on business before he could start digging at Troy.

His business in America took longer than he had expected. While he was there he became an American citizen, then he divorced his wife, Catherine, who refused to share his life. At last he was free to think about Troy again.

In spite of his wealth Henry was a very lonely man. All his life he had longed for companionship and affection. He wished particularly for a wife who would share his love of old cities and his wish to dig up the remains of Troy. From now on he meant to live mainly in Greece.

'Perhaps a Greek wife would be the best helpmate for me,' he told himself, 'but this time she must be the right kind of woman and as interested in the old things as I am. Perhaps Vimpos could advise me. He is a wise man.'

His old friend Vimpos had now become Archbishop of Athens. Henry wrote to him and begged his help in choosing a wife.

'I do not care if she is poor, but she must be well educated. She must love Homer and the old things of her country. Above all, she must have a good and loving heart. Perhaps you know an orphan, the daughter of a scholarly man? If possible I would like her to be black-haired and beautiful.'

This may seem to us a strange way of choosing a wife. In the countries of the Near East it was the custom for marriages to be arranged between families. To the Archbishop there was nothing unusual about Henry's request. He immediately considered all the young women of his family. There was his cousin's daughter, Sophia. She was an intelligent, beautiful girl who was training to be a teacher. Sophia was young, only seventeen years of age, but she had plenty of common sense. Vimpos consulted her parents and sent her photograph to Henry Schliemann.

Henry took the first possible ship across the Atlantic to Athens. When he arrived at the house Sophia's parents, brothers, sisters, even cousins, were all there to receive him

The Plain of Troy

according to the Greek custom. Sophia came into the room looking very beautiful indeed in a white dress, with white ribbons in her hair. She had a sweet serious expression that Henry liked at once. He wanted to be sure, though, that she had the kind of mind he desired. He talked to the family of his travels, then turned to Sophia, 'Would you like to go on long journeys?' he asked.

Sophia replied that she would be very happy to do so.

The next question he asked was to test Sophia's knowledge of history. 'When did the Emperor Hadrian visit Athens?'

Sophia gave him the exact date.

His third question was, 'What passages from Homer do you know by heart?'

Sophia recited a passage to him and Henry was satisfied.

Here was the wife for him! A month later they were married.

Both Vimpos and Schliemann were right. Strange though the courtship was, and though Henry was many years older than Sophia, she was the right wife for him. Their married life was one of understanding and abiding love. She proved his companion and helpmate in all his work and she went with him to dig out the ruins of ancient cities. Once again Henry had been wonderfully lucky.

The next year Henry Schliemann went to Hissarlik to try to find what was left of the ancient city of Troy. This time he did not take Sophia with him. She had been ill when they were in Paris and he left her with her family in Athens. She was to join him when it could be arranged.

At Hissarlik he employed ten Turkish labourers who began to dig the western part of the mound overlooking the sea. After an hour's digging they came on the remains of a wall two feet below the surface. By nightfall they had bared the foundations of a large building. Henry was very excited when they uncovered flagstones, though he did not think these were the flagstones of the city of Troy before the days of Homer, when Priam was king there. These stones belonged to buildings of a later date. All the same, Henry was sure that below these buildings he would come on other buildings of more ancient time. He decided to cut a trench right across the middle of the mound to see if his guess was correct. At a depth of fifteen feet he came on walls six feet thick. Below these were yet other walls nine feet thick. Henry felt sure he was getting near the walls of ancient Troy.

Before he could get any further he had trouble with the Turks who owned the land. Henry offered to buy it, but the Turkish men insisted they needed it for their sheep grazing. Even when he came to an agreement with them he still had to get permission to dig there from the Turkish government. This was very hard to obtain.

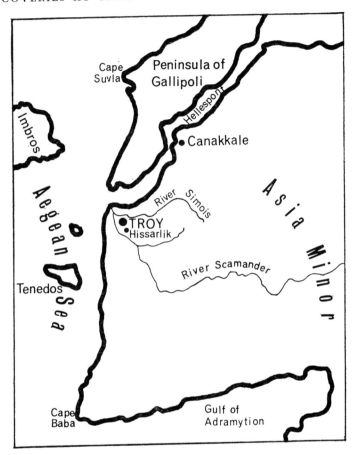

Sketch map showing Troy

Dismayed but not defeated, Henry returned home. He remembered he was now an American citizen and begged the American ambassador in Constantinople to try to get a permit for him. At last, after much waiting, the permit was granted. As soon as it could be arranged Henry and Sophia hurried to Troy. Now he could go ahead with the digging. Already it was August and the rainy season was near.

He started digging with eight workmen but within two
or three days he was employing seventy-four men. He had
a faithful Greek servant, Jannakis, whom he could trust.
Jannakis managed the workmen for him and saw to paying
their wages.

In October they began to find hundreds of small clay
objects and polished stones like lance heads. There were little
clay models of owls, and tiles with an owl's head upon them.
They found little else of value but, as they went deeper into
the ground, they found walls of huge blocks of stone and
a doorway with a door-sill. Henry was more sure than ever
that he had reached the walls of ancient Troy.

The next year, 1872, Henry and Sophia went back to
Hissarlik again. This time he was heartened by the gift of
sixty wheelbarrows, spades and picks from Schroeders. It did
Henry good to think that at least his old company believed
in him and in Troy.

The workmen cut deep trenches across the mound. They
came upon more huge walls, but still no proof that they had
reached the ancient city of King Priam. Then in June a
wonderful stone carving was unearthed. It showed the Greek
god Apollo in his chariot drawn by the four horses of the
sun.

This encouraged Henry a great deal, but the summer
heat began to try him, wiry man though he was. Still he
toiled on, then just as he was about to give up digging in
August, he found his first treasure.

'We've come on a skeleton, the skeleton of a woman,' he
told Sophia. 'Look what we found among her bones.' He
held out his hand. In it were three very old earrings and a gold
brooch.

They laboured on, hoping for still more treasure but found
nothing. Suddenly the rains came. There were heavy
thunderstorms and the trenches were turned into streams of

mud. They had to give up digging and return to Athens.

What Henry had found made him sure there must still be objects to unearth. Next spring early in 1873 he was back on the job with Sophia beside him.

Henry built a wooden house on the site. The March winds blew through the cracks. The nights were cold, even freezing, but the heat in the day time rose rapidly to over 70° Fahrenheit.

Henry wrote in his diary, 'For the past fortnight we have been hearing the croaking of millions of frogs. At night there is the hideous screeching of many owls that nest around us. There is something weird and horrible about their screeching; it is unbearable, especially at night.'

Perhaps it was as well that Henry's sleep was disturbed by the owls. Towards the end of March he woke one morning at 3 a.m. coughing and choking. The room was full of dense smoke. The floor-boards and the wall by the fireplace were beginning to blaze.

'Wake up, Sophia!' he yelled, shaking her by the shoulder. 'Get out of here quickly! Wake Jannakis! Tell him to come and help me.'

Jannakis slept in a nearby hut.

Luckily there was a bath of water lying in the hut. Henry flung it over the blazing boards. Jannakis joined him and seized a barrow-load of earth and spades which had been left standing outside. They shovelled the earth over the flames till they were extinguished. This was the second time Henry had escaped death by fire as well as twice by drowning! Shuddering and pale with horror he exclaimed, 'If I had slept even a minute longer the whole house might have been destroyed!'

Sophia looked horrified too. 'To think we might have lost the precious things we have dug out with so much toil, and all your diaries and papers too!'

'That would not have been the worst. I might have lost *you*, Sophia! You might have perished in the flames. Life is nothing for me without you. There can be no digging for Troy unless you are by my side,' he declared. Henry knew that in Sophia he had the dearest treasure of all.

In April the keen winds died down and the plain of Troy was covered with spring flowers. Henry found hope rising strongly in him. 'I feel we are close to great discoveries,' he told Sophia.

It was as though he could see into the future, for soon the diggers unearthed a paved street. In a nearby stone building they came on nine earthenware jars, big enough for a man to stand inside them.

'Most likely they held grain or oil,' Henry decided. 'It makes the story seem quite possible of Ali Baba and the Forty Thieves who hid in great jars like these.'

In May they made further discoveries. The labourers dug out two great stone gates twenty feet apart and the remains of a large house behind the gates. The house bore the marks of having been destroyed by fire. Inside it many vases of all sizes were found. Henry became very excited.

'I am sure this is the Scaean Gate mentioned by Homer. This great house must have been King Priam's palace,' he decided. 'We have found the Troy of Homer's stories at last! I have discovered what I set out to find.'

Henry Schliemann was feeling very tired and the weather was becoming very hot. 'It will soon be too warm for us to dig,' he told Sophia. 'We will go on till the end of May, but when June comes we shall have to pack up and go back to Athens. I have reached the great goal of my life in finding Troy. Later on, perhaps, I will dig in Greece, may be among the ruins of Mycenae.'

'Do you think there is no more to discover here, then?' Sophia asked.

'Oh, there is *much* more yet to find out about these ruined and buried cities, perhaps even Priam's treasure buried here, but best of all will be the knowledge we shall find of these lost civilizations.' Henry Schliemann knew that true archaeologists dug, not specially for golden treasure, but for *knowledge*. This was far more important. All the same, treasure did come his way.

Two weeks later, towards the end of May, a few workmen were digging along the city wall joined to the Scaean Gate. Suddenly a bright gleam caught Henry's eye. He peered among the dust and rubble at the foot of the wall. The gleam came from what seemed to be a large copper cauldron of oblong shape, almost like a copper chest. Henry thought that, in the gap, he could see two helmets on top of it and there were also articles piled inside the cauldron. Was this Priam's treasure?

Henry glanced around. The workmen were busy digging along the trench. No one but Henry had noticed the gleam of the metal. He thought quickly. If it was indeed the treasure it would be as well if the workmen knew nothing about it. They were a tough crew and Henry thought they might not stop short of robbing him. There was the observer, too, sent by the Turkish Government to keep an eye on what Henry dug up. Henry had no intention of his sharing in any discoveries. He called Sophia to him, put a finger to his lips, then said, 'Go at once to the men and tell them they can stop work. Tell them it is a rest period, anything you like!'

'But it's only seven o'clock in the morning! They have not been working for an hour yet.' Sophia was amazed.

'All the same, go and tell them to stop! Make up any story you like. Tell them it's my birthday and they can keep it as a holiday.'

'Your birthday?' Sophia looked bewildered.

'Yes. Say I have just remembered it and they may have a holiday in honour of it. Tell them every man will get his full wages for the day. Only see to it that they all go away to their homes and the Turkish overseer goes with them! Then come back here to me.'

Sophia guessed there must be a reason for his extraordinary behaviour and she hastened to obey him.

Though the men were astonished, the thought of an unexpected holiday on full pay was very welcome, though the Turkish overseer looked a bit puzzled as he walked away. Still, if there were no workmen there, there could be no digging, he reasoned with himself. 'No digging, no need to watch for discoveries!' He shrugged his shoulders and hastened home too.

When the workmen were gone, Sophia returned to her husband.

'Look there!' He pointed to the foot of the wall where he had seen the copper gleam.

Sophia knelt down in the trench and peered at the copper vessel. The side of it was broken and through the hole there came the glint of silver and golden objects. On the top of the cauldron burnt rubble was packed together tightly by the weight of the wall above it. Once again Henry was certain he had come on the burned city of Homer's story. He began to scrape with a knife at the rubble round the cauldron to loosen it.

'Do be careful!' Sophia begged him. 'It would only require a careless movement to make the wall cave in on top of you.'

All the same, she got a knife and shovel for herself and knelt and worked alongside him. Very slowly and carefully they moved the rubble from round the vessel, then gently prised out the copper cauldron from the wall. Henry began to lift out metal objects from it.

'They're *gold*!' he exclaimed in an amazed whisper. 'Go

fetch your big shawl, Sophia.'

Sophia hastened to the wooden house to fetch her big scarlet shawl. One by one Henry laid the treasures from the copper cauldron on to the shawl, then Sophia bundled them up. The burden was heavy to lift but they managed it between them. When they reached the ladder out of the trench Henry carried the bundle over his shoulder and Sophia came behind and steadied it. At last they reached their hut, dragged the bundle in and locked the door, breathing hard.

Henry spread the treasure out on the bare wooden table. Sophia caught her breath when she saw it. 'Oh, Henry, can it be true?' she faltered.

'We've found it at last! We've found the treasure of Priam!' Henry exulted, lifting up a silver vase and two golden cups.

'Whoever hid it away did it carefully. Look! All the big cups and vases have smaller things stowed away inside them,' Sophia pointed out.

Inside three big silver vases they found two gold diadems, a gold head-band, four long, dangling, gold ear-rings, fifty-six smaller ear-rings and nearly *nine thousand* gold rings and buttons. All day they spent sorting and counting the articles.

'It's like a jeweller's shop!' Sophia exclaimed.

Henry picked up a diadem made of nearly a hundred golden chains with pendants and tassels and held it up to the light. 'I have never seen anything like this before!' he declared. 'Look how it glows in the sunlight! Come here, Sophia!'

He placed the diadem on Sophia's dark lustrous hair and stood back to look at her.

'Not even Helen of Troy was lovelier than you are now, Sophia,' he told her in a whisper. 'You are wearing the jewels of a queen. Who knows? Perhaps they were last worn by Helen of Troy when men went to war for her?'

Suddenly Sophia gave a little shudder. She felt she could not wear the jewels any longer, even to please Henry. 'What shall we do with all this treasure?' she asked practically. 'We cannot keep it in the hut or it might be stolen.'

'If the Turkish overseer casts his eyes upon it he will seize it and send it to Constantinople. And what will they do with it there?' Henry's voice rose excitedly. 'I know the Turks. They will melt it down for the sake of the gold and then these priceless treasures will be lost for ever.'

'What will you do with them, then?' Sophia asked.

'When I have had time to examine all the things and write about them and draw them for the book I shall write, then I will give them to some great museum. *I* found them, so it must be my right to decide which museum shall have them. It must be a museum to which the whole world can come and look at them.'

Sophia had to bring Henry back to earth again. 'Yes, but we have first to get them out of here. How shall we do that?'

Henry thought hard. 'The Turkish overseer is hardly likely to let us whisk them away under his very nose. They must leave here tonight, as soon as it is dark. Frank Calvert is the man who will help us. I can trust him. He will manage to smuggle the treasure to Athens for us.'

They packed the treasure into boxes and a sack. As soon as darkness had fallen they put the treasure on a wheelbarrow and trundled it over the deserted lanes to Frank Calvert's house. His eyes almost popped out of his head when he saw what was in the boxes and sack.

'I am convinced it is King Priam's treasure that he hid when Troy was sacked and burned by his enemies,' Henry told him.

'It may not have been Priam's, but there is no doubt that it is a priceless treasure,' Calvert agreed. He put it carefully away in a big iron-banded chest and locked the lid down. 'You take the key,' he said to Schliemann. 'Tomorrow I will make arrangements to send the chest by ship to Athens.'

Perhaps Amin Effendi, the Turkish overseer, had had time to wonder about the unexpected holiday and feel there was something suspicious about it, for next day he arrived at Schliemann's house. 'I think you are hiding something from me,' he said. 'I wish to enter your house and examine what you have in your boxes.'

'You have no right to search our dwelling,' Henry told him, 'but you may come in and look round and satisfy yourself.'

The scene of Schliemann's excavations at Hissarlik
From the Illustrated London News, *29 December 1877*

In the boxes Amin Effendi found small clay figures and vases but no gold!

Frank Calvert managed to ship the treasure secretly to Athens. As soon as Henry Schliemann got word it was safely on its way he decided to pay off his men and return home with Sophia. Once they were back in Athens, Henry and Sophia had a busy time examining the treasure and making lists with descriptions and drawings of the objects. Then the treasures were carefully wrapped in straw and placed in boxes.

'What shall we do with them now?' Henry asked. 'It will not do to keep these things here in case the Turks demand that the Greek government send them back to Turkey.'

Sophia had a plan in her head. She invited many of her trusted relations to visit them. As Greek people are fond of big family gatherings, no one guessed the purpose of these visits.

'Will you do something to help us?' Sophia asked each one. 'Here is part of the treasure my husband brought away from Troy. Will you take it with you and hide it somewhere safe in your house?'

Each one who went away after a visit carried a basket or a parcel. One took away a vase stuffed with golden rings; another had a golden diadem hidden beneath fruit in a basket. The treasure disappeared as if by magic!

Henry was now able to write an account of his digging at Troy and the things he had found there and to send it to different countries. He was able to tell the world how he had proved that Homer told the truth and wrote history, not folk-lore; that Troy was *real*.

The Turkish government claimed the treasure and even searched the house in Athens to try to find it, but of course it had vanished. There was a long dispute which ended in the law courts in Athens. At last the affair was settled and Henry paid the Turkish Government a large sum of money for the

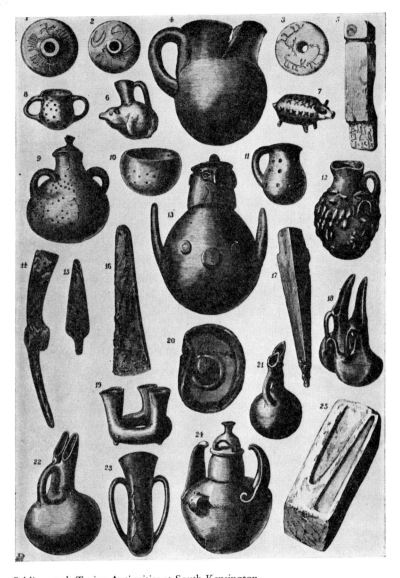

Schliemann's Trojan Antiquities at South Kensington

*1, 2, 3. 'Whorls' with sacred emblems. 4. Silver jug, which contained trinkets. 5. Whetstone.
6, 7. Terra-cotta animals. 8–11. Perforated pottery. 12. Terra-cotta jug. 13. Minerva vase.
14–17. Axe, dagger, axe, lance, all of bronze. 18. Double jug of terra-cotta. 19. Three-spouted
terra-cotta vessel. 20. Copper shield. 21, 22. Terra-cotta jugs. 23, 24. Terra-cotta vases. 25. Slate
mould for casting bronze weapons.*

share of the treasure which was theirs. He was satisfied, for he had got what he wanted; the right to keep for himself the priceless treasure he had unearthed.

'Some day I shall give it all to a museum so that the whole world may come and look at it,' he told Sophia.

'Which museum?' Sophia asked.

'That I have not yet decided. I shall take my time in thinking about it.'

The treasure remained hidden in the many houses and farms of Sophia's family.

Not long afterwards, Henry and Sophia, taking with them their little daughter, went on a tour of the great cities of Europe to give lectures about Troy to learned societies. They came to London where they had great honours heaped upon them. Queen Victoria received them; they visited Mr Gladstone, the Prime Minister, who became a great friend of Schliemann's and actually wrote an introduction to Schliemann's book. It seemed hardly possible that Henry was the boy who had once slept under the grocer's counter, with never a penny to his name. He had come a long way indeed.

All London thronged to hear his lectures. Sophia spoke, too, in her careful and precise English. When she described how they had found the treasure, she won everybody's heart.

'What a remarkable woman she is! She's beautiful and she's modest too!' were the remarks on everyone's lips.

At one of their lectures a schoolboy sat entranced. He listened to every word they said with rapt attention. When they had finished, he heaved a deep sigh as one who had come out of a dream. The boy was Arthur Evans. One day he was to travel in Henry Schliemann's footsteps and go to Greece and the lovely islands off its shores. In particular he was to visit Crete. One day he was to take up Henry Schliemann's work there where he had left it unfinished.

CHAPTER FOUR

○○○

'Mycenae, Rich in Gold'

In his poem, the *Iliad*, Homer tells how the Achaeans (Greeks) went to do battle at Troy to win back the beautiful Helen, wife of Menelaus, King of Sparta, who had been stolen away by a Trojan prince, Paris. Commanding the Greek forces was Agamemnon, King of Mycenae, the richest and most powerful king in Greece.

Mycenae was a great fortress standing on a hill top, crowned by the palace of King Agamemnon. It was to this palace that Agamemnon returned victorious after his long wars against Troy. His wife, Clytemnestra, hated him and plotted with one of his noblemen to kill Agamemnon at the banquet held to celebrate the homecoming of the warriors. This terrible deed was carried out. It sparked off a battle about which Homer says, 'Not a single man of the king's soldiers was left, nor of Aegisthus's company either. They were killed in the palace to a man.'

A later writer than Homer, Pausanius, wrote: 'In the ruins of Mycenae there is the tomb of Agamemnon. Clytemnestra and Aegisthus were buried a little outside the wall because they were thought unworthy of burial within it, where Agamemnon lies and those who were killed with him.'

135

Henry Schliemann gave a great deal of thought to this ancient tragedy. He thought, too, of Homer's writing of 'Mycenae, rich in gold'. He tried to work out where the tombs of these people might be found. Already tombs had been discovered at the foot of the hill of Mycenae where the old city had nestled below the fortress. Most people thought that 'the wall' mentioned by Pausanius meant the wall encircling the lower city and that Agamemnon's tomb was among those uncovered and robbed in far-off time. Henry did not agree with this.

'I do not think Pausanius meant the wall of the city at all,' he told Sophia. 'I think he meant the great *inner* wall of the fortress. It was far more likely that Agamemnon would be buried inside the wall of his own castle.'

'What makes you so sure which wall Pausanius meant?' Sophia asked.

'Because Pausanius mentions the Gateway of the Lions. That is the gateway into the fortress. I am sure the tombs of Agamemnon and his faithful bodyguard must be inside the wall of the citadel and that in the tombs we shall find this king, even if there is no treasure of gold.'

'Are we to dig next at Mycenae, then?' Sophia enquired with an understanding smile.

'Yes. I shall dig inside the Gateway of the Lions. It was near the gateway of Troy that I found the treasure of gold. Perhaps the same thing may happen at Mycenae.'

Henry had to wait a long time before he got permission from the Greek government to dig at Mycenae. They made it a condition that his digging was to be watched by one of their officials. Henry was very annoyed, because he had already promised to hand over to them any treasure he found in Greece. He hated being 'spied upon' and plagued by officials.

In August 1876 Schliemann began digging just inside the

Gate of the Lions at Mycenae. He employed sixty-three workmen from nearby villages. Before long he came on many vases and fragments of pottery, bronze knives and arrow heads. He and Sophia watched the diggers all the time. So did Stamatakis, the watcher for the Greek government. It was terribly hot and tiring in the blazing sun. Henry wrote

The Lion Gate, Mycenae

in his diary: 'Mrs Schliemann and I superintend the excavations from morning till dusk. We suffer severely from the scorching sun and incessant tempest which blows the dust into our eyes and inflames them. In spite of these annoyances nothing more interesting can be imagined than the excavation of a prehistoric city of immortal glory where nearly every object reveals a new page of history.'

By September he had 125 workmen on the job. He was having constant quarrels with the Greek 'watcher', Stamatakis, who objected to the pulling down of walls to reach the remains of an earlier city that Henry was sure lay buried beneath them.

'I shall give up the digging and leave Greece altogether!' Henry threatened. 'Does the Greek government realize I am paying for all this digging out of my own pocket?'

Sophia had no wish to leave Greece. When the quarrels grew fierce she would step in and speak a few calming sensible words to both sides. Strange to say, both men listened to her and the work went on.

At first they found little of value, then, in mid-September, the workmen who were digging just south of the Lion Gate came upon two carved tombstones. One showed a hunter chasing a deer; the second bore a warrior in a chariot and the horse being attacked by a soldier.

Next they uncovered a circle of stone slabs.

'This must have been the *Agora* or Meeting Place,' Henry said.

He might have begun to dig there at once, but nearby he found the walls of what seemed to have been a large house. 'This could have been the King's palace,' Henry surmised.

Among fragments of pottery he came on one great discovery. This was part of a vase about twelve inches high. On it were six warriors painted in a dark red colour on a light yellow ground. It seemed as if they were marching to battle

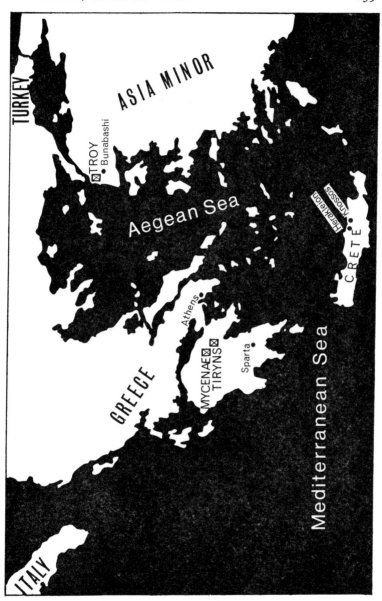

The sites of Schliemann's excavations

carrying their long spears and semi-circular shields. They
wore coats of mail and horned helmets with plumed crests.
A woman was waving them farewell. They marched with
a kind of light prancing step. Henry handled the vase with
great tenderness. 'These might have been the men of
Mycenae setting out for the Trojan war,' he said.

It is possible he was right about that. Henry again began
to feel he was on the verge of new and exciting discoveries.
Little else of interest turned up in the house, so in October
Henry began to dig up the *Agora* or ancient Meeting Place
just inside the gate. Then, indeed, exciting events began to
happen.

The diggers came on a big tomb, but robbers had already
plundered it. Only a few gold buttons were found scattered
on the ground. Henry ordered the digging to go on. At
fifteen feet below the surface he reached a layer of pebbles.

'These pebbles did not come there of themselves. They
must have been put there by human hands,' he reasoned.
'Move them and dig under them.'

Almost at once they came on the remains of three human
bodies thickly covered with clay and ashes from a funeral
fire. The spade had stripped some clay from one of the bodies
and through the gap came the glint of gold.

'We can use the spades no longer. Here we must work
carefully and strip away the clay with knives, a little at a
time. Nothing must be destroyed,' Henry ordered.

When Henry went down into the tomb to begin the
scraping, he found he was too excited and impatient to handle
the knife gently.

'I . . . I'm afraid to tackle the job. It's too delicate for me,'
he told Sophia.

'Give me the knife. I will do it,' Sophia offered.

'*You* will, Sophia?'

'Yes. It is a task better suited to a woman's hand.'

She was right. It called for a steadier hand than Henry's, a hand more delicate in the touch. Gruesome though the work was of scraping the soil from the bones of long dead warriors, Sophia carried on patiently with it. There was nothing she would not do to help Henry. For twenty-five days she worked on her knees at the bottom of the tomb, scraping away the soil in fine layers. All the time Stamatakis watched and so did Schliemann. Then, at last, she began to hand out the beautiful golden objects she found on each body.

Each man had been buried with five golden diadems or crowns. These diadems were different from the ones they found at Troy. Those had been made of many chains. The Mycenean ones were made of sheets of gold hammered very thin. They had been stamped with beautiful patterns of circles and lines, the circles growing smaller as they reached the sides of the diadems. On two of the bodies Sophia found five gold ornaments made in the shape of laurel leaves crossed. The third body had four of these leaves. Here was treasure indeed, priceless treasure of gold!

Every night Sophia and Henry carried the treasures in a basket to the house where they were staying in the nearby village of Chavati. Every night the objects of gold and fragments of pottery and the weapons were counted, numbered and locked away by Schliemann and Stamatakis.

Schliemann went on digging in the same circle of graves. He found more bodies but no treasure. All the same some sixth sense told him to keep on digging there. Then indeed he came on a treasure beyond his wildest dreams.

He uncovered another tomb which again held three bodies. Henry thought, because they were smaller, that they were the bodies of women.

'The bodies were laden with jewels and gold', Henry wrote in his diary. 'One of the women had a magnificent gold crown on her head.' This splendid diadem was hammered with designs in circles and all along the top edge were thirty-six ornamental leaves which stood upright.

What astonished Henry and Sophia most, however, were the thick gold discs scattered all over the floor of the tomb like round gold leaves. Every disc was ornamented in hammered designs; some with circle patterns, some with flower petals, some with cuttlefish and some with butterflies. There were also leaf patterns. They were exquisitely made. Henry himself picked up over *seven hundred* of them from the ground around the bodies.

Among the ornaments found with the bones were necklaces, pendants, golden clasps to hold the hair, a gold comb, an enormous quantity of amber beads, a golden flower on a silver stalk and two silver sceptres plated with gold. Again they found crosses of laurel leaves lying on the bodies and they wondered what strange significance they might have.

It was Sophia who once more went down on her knees beside the bodies and patiently scraped away the soil with a knife, uncovering these treasures.

Henry Schliemann was not yet satisfied that he had discovered all the burials within the *Agora*, the circle bounded by the stone slabs.

'I shall keep on digging within the *Agora*,' he told Sophia.

'It is a big place to dig entirely. Have you any particular part in mind?' Sophia asked.

'Yes, I have. I noticed that just to the west of the third grave the colour of the soil is different. It is black earth, much darker than the rest of the soil elsewhere. Unlike the other parts of the site, I think it must never have been disturbed. We will see what is below it.'

The diggers went to work. Twenty feet below the surface they came on a circular mass of stone with a round opening in the middle like a well. Henry guessed what it was.

'I think it is a kind of altar. Into the opening in the centre men used to pour offerings of oil and wine to the spirits of the dead. There must be a burial somewhere very near, perhaps even below the altar.'

Henry had the altar lifted and, sure enough, they came on two slabs like tomb-stones which they removed. About four feet below the slabs Henry found a huge burial chamber. It was twenty-four feet long and eighteen feet broad and hewn out of the solid rock. The bottom of the tomb was covered with a layer of pebbles. On these pebbles, placed at equal distances from each other, were the bodies of five men. They had been covered with a layer of four inches of white clay, which, of course, had hardened. The bodies must have been those of kings and warriors, for a heap of more than twenty bronze swords and many lances were found lying near the bodies.

Henry writes in his diary: 'From this point we have had to do the work ourselves; the task is extremely difficult and painful for us, particularly in the present rainy weather, for we cannot dig otherwise than on our knees and by cutting the earth and stones carefully away with our knives, so as not to injure or lose any of the gold ornaments.'

To Sophia, of course, fell the work of stripping the hardened clay from the bodies, particularly from the faces, where her light deft fingers could work most delicately. Henry, too, helped her where possible.

As Sophia worked, patiently scraping a thin film of clay away from the head of one of the skeletons, she gave a startled exclamation. 'Look, Henry! There's a *face* here!'

'A face!' Amazed, Henry hurried to her.

'See! A face of gold!'

Henry peered over her shoulder. 'Scrape a bit more there.'

'I cannot hurry the work. This calls for greater care than ever.'

At last Sophia uncovered the face of the dead man. It

proved to be a mask of thin beaten gold, showing his features quite plainly.

'This must have been some great king,' Henry said in awe, 'Nothing like this golden mask has ever been seen before.'

This was not the last of the astonishing finds. Four of the bodies wore these wonderful golden masks. They were all different in appearance.

'They are death masks. They must have been modelled by an artist when each man lay dead, for there is the stamp of death upon them,' Henry declared. 'But they are the likenesses of the dead men, for every one is different. They have a strange and frightening beauty.'

They also found a golden mask in the shape of a lion's head. Possibly this was worn in some ritual ceremonies. Two golden signet rings were also found by the hands. These rings bore intaglios, or pictures, engraved on a flat gold surface of the ring. One of the intaglios bore a hunting scene, the other a battle scene. Copper vessels containing golden buttons were also found. Then Henry came on a very strange discovery indeed.

'I found a cow's head of silver with two golden horns', he wrote in his diary. 'There was a splendidly ornamented golden sun on its forehead. There was also two other cows' heads of very thin gold plate *which have a double axe between the horns.*'

These finds plainly puzzled Henry. Had he but known it, these animals' heads, which were bulls and not cows, together with the double axe heads, the picture of the warrior on the vase, the intaglios on the rings, were all valuable clues to the history of the Mediterranean peoples. Similar rings with intaglios, double axe-heads, gold and silver bulls' horns were found years later by Sir Arthur Evans in Crete. These showed there was a strong Cretan influence on the art of Mycenae. Certainly the Mycenaens had traded with Crete and obtained goods from there. It is even possible that Cretan artists worked in Greece. Without doubt there was a great coming and going between Mycenae and Crete in those far off times. Later on Henry Schliemann had another opportunity of finding out more about the Cretans and their association with the Mycenaens, but he lost it due to ill chance. It fell to Arthur Evans, the boy who had attended Henry and Sophia's lecture in London, to take up the clues which Henry had missed.

Gold mask found by Schliemann at Mycenae

Arthur Evans believed that the Cretans had at one time conquered the Mycenaens but later archaeologists have declared him wrong. Their close association is more likely to have been by way of trade.

Henry was almost overwhelmed by the mass of treasure found in this grave. Besides the golden masks, two of the bodies wore golden breast-plates. He also found eleven solid gold cups and goblets. Henry wrote: 'One of these goblets vividly reminds us of Nestor's cup mentioned in the *Iliad*, for it has two golden doves modelled upon the handles.'

Indeed, it was almost exactly like the cup Homer had described in the *Iliad*. Once more Henry felt his deep belief in Homer as an historian had been proved correct.

'I *must* go on digging,' he told Sophia. 'I must find everything there is to find at Mycenae. I still think we did not dig deep enough in the first grave we opened in the *Agora*.'

They had been stopped there from further digging by the rains and the mud the rains had caused.

Sure enough, Henry's instinct led him right once more! It was this grave which, for him, yielded the treasure that mattered most. Under a layer of pebbles they found three more bodies. The third wore a beautiful mask of gold. Under the mask the round face had been wonderfully preserved, showing the man almost as he had been in life. The face was that of a man about thirty-five years old, with thirty-two beautiful teeth. The body was covered with a golden breast-plate. When Henry looked again at the very regal mask on the *first* skeleton, however, he jumped to a conclusion. 'This must be King Agamemnon!' he cried. 'Agamemnon who went to war against the Trojans more than 3,000 years ago!'

Homer wrote about him in the *Iliad*, 'King Agamemnon led the troops that came from the great stronghold of Mycenae. He was a proud man as he took his stand with his people, armed in gleaming bronze, the greatest captain of all.'

Henry Schliemann was overcome with joy. This was the crowning glory of his discoveries. He looked at the golden mask with reverence. 'I have gazed on the face of Agamemnon!' he cried in triumph.

The mask indeed showed a face of majesty and power. The eyes were closed but the lips seemed to smile. Was it indeed the death mask of the mighty Agamemnon?

In later years other archaeologists proved that Henry Schliemann was mistaken. This indeed was the body of a king, but one who had lived long before Agamemnon. The triumph and glory of the discovery were no less.

'We have finished here,' Henry told Sophia. 'The work is done. We will go back to Athens and write about these things we have found.'

They spent the winter in Athens and Henry Schliemann wrote his book and illustrated it with photographs and drawings of the wonderful treasures he had found. He translated the book into French and English, and begged William Gladstone, who was the British Prime Minister, and admired his work very much, to write an introduction to it. Gladstone wrote quite a long preface to Henry Schliemann's book.

Yet another joy was in store for Henry Schliemann. Later that year Sophia had a son. It seemed like a dream come true when Henry gave the name Agamemnon to his Greek son. He decided to build a beautiful house in Athens for Sophia and his children. He made it a model of the palaces he had imagined in Troy and Mycenae, a huge house with marble steps and pillars, tiled floors and friezes of the Greek heroes on the walls.

Henry had promised to give the treasure of Mycenae to Greece and he kept his promise. It can be seen today in the great national museum of Athens, a glittering splendour of gold under the glass cases.

We must remember that Henry Schliemann did not dig up this great treasure of gold to keep for himself. He wished it to be placed in a museum so that people could see it for themselves and learn more about the great race of Mycenaeans. No *real* archaeologist digs just to unearth treasure, but he digs for *knowledge*, to know more about the history of mankind.

○○

Tiryns and Crete

Even the treasures of Mycenae did not satisfy Schliemann's thirst for discovery. He went back to Troy again to dig out the lost cities. This time he took with him an assistant, William Dorpfeld, a young German. William was a clever surveyor and architect and he made an excellent map of Troy, with drawings to show the different layers of the cities which had been built. They found seven in all which had been buried in the mound of Hissarlik. Later excavation by Dorpfeld added two more. There had been nine cities in all built on the site of Troy.

Henry began to consider other places where he might dig up ancient cities. He remembered Tiryns, a ruined city near the Gulf of Nauplia, not far from Mycenae. It was a great fortress built on a crag overlooking the sea. Schliemann wrote, 'It was not till March 1884 that I was able to realize my long-deferred hope of exploring Tiryns'.

He took William Dorpfeld with him. Henry was to look for pottery and ornaments but Dorpfeld was to be the surveyor and map-maker of the great walls. This time Sophia remained in Athens to look after her young family.

Schliemann and Dorpfeld stayed at an hotel in Nauplia

about three miles away from Tiryns. The farmhouse near Tiryns which they had hoped to occupy was too tumbledown and dirty. Every morning Henry rose before 4 o'clock and was rowed out to sea in a small boat. He plunged overboard and had a brisk swim for ten minutes, then returned to Nauplia, dressed and had a cup of black coffee. He went to Tiryns on horseback and was busy watching the workmen excavating by 6 o'clock. At 8 o'clock everyone had a break-fast-break and he and Dorpfeld sat on a stone in the shade of a wall and ate bread and corned beef, cheese and oranges.

First of all the men had to clear away the soil and rubbish that covered the ruins. By midsummer they had laid bare the foundations of an immense stone palace built of huge blocks. No other fortress in Greece had such strong walls. No doubt they had remained standing because the blocks of stone were too big and heavy to be carried off to build houses and farms in the district after the palace had become a ruin.

Tiryns must have been a most impressive palace. 'The home of a great prehistoric king', Schliemann wrote of it. There was a men's court approached by a stately ante-room; there was also a women's court with many rooms opening off it. There was even a bathroom.

Henry was delighted to find the bathroom, for Homer had described one just like it. The floor was made of one huge slab of stone. The water ran off from it into a square-cut gutter which led to a pipe. This pipe carried the water outside to a drain. The very ancient people who had lived at Tiryns evidently knew something of plumbing. In a corner of the bathroom stood the fragments of what had once been a terracotta bath-tub. Terracotta is made of clay and baked in kilns like bricks or pottery. This bath-tub had handles and was decorated with painted patterns. Many years later, in the palace of Knossos on the island of Crete, Arthur Evans dug out a similar bathroom.

Henry found no treasure of gold at Tiryns such as he had found at Mycenae and Troy, but he dug out beautifully shaped vases and bowls, some of which may have been hung up as oil lamps, for they had perforations through which strings could be threaded for hanging.

Probably the men's court and the women's court had been decorated by frescoes or wall paintings. The walls had had a plastering of clay to make them smooth. Over this, lime had been washed. On this surface the painting was done. Much

Ruins of the great fortress at Tiryns

of the plaster had fallen from the walls and lay in large fragments. On these fragments were painted gay patterns and pictures. The most astounding was one of a bull.

On a frieze a mighty bull with long curved horns ran wildly. His eye was ferocious and glaring. Above the back of the beast was a man kneeling on one knee with his right hand clutching the bull's horns. He had evidently leaped on

Gold cups discovered near Sparta; they show bull motifs such as Schliemann noted at Tiryns . . .

to the back of the bull and was doing some acrobatic trick. The figure of the man was painted white against a blue ground and the bull was also white but decorated with red spots. Many of the fragments of these frescoes and some beautiful pottery is to be seen today in the museum at Tiryns.

Though Henry did not realize it at the time, the fresco was one of the most valuable finds he made. When Arthur

... and that later were found on frescoes at Knossos and on Crete

Evans dug out the old palace of Knossos in Crete he found a similar fresco of a charging bull. The frescoes at Tiryns and those of Crete had similar subjects, though the style of painting was different. It pointed to much coming and going between the two countries by trade and possibly even by war. The bull's head of gold and the fresco at Tiryns showed that these people held the bull as a sacred animal. No doubt young men, and very likely young women too, were trained to do acrobatic tricks on the back of a bull. These young people were probably slaves carried off in war from other countries. Sooner or later they would be gored by the bull, perhaps when they were performing on a feast day before the eyes of the crowd. This was regarded as a sacrifice to the sacred bull.

Henry Schliemann was beginning to have an inkling that the discoveries at Mycenae and Tiryns were connected with Crete and that there was a link between them all.

'I should like to go to Crete. I am convinced that rewarding discoveries could be made there,' he told Dorpfeld, who agreed with him.

Accordingly in 1886 they went to Crete and examined the site of the ancient palace of Knossos.

'The pottery here is very like that I found at Tiryns,' Henry pointed out. 'We will make arrangements to dig here.'

The government of Crete was willing that Schliemann should excavate at Knossos provided that he handed over to them all the treasures he might find. They were to be placed in a museum at Heraklion, the chief town of Crete.

When all seemed set fair for Schliemann to go ahead with the digging at Knossos they suffered a bad set-back. The farmer who owned the land would not sell by itself the part where the ruins lay. He wanted to sell the whole hillside and all the olive trees on it. He asked about £5,000 for his fields.

Henry regarded this as an outrageous price and he refused to pay it and went back to Athens.

For three years Henry and the farmer haggled about the price, then the farmer agreed to sell the fields for about half the price he had formerly asked. Henry at once took ship for Crete. He found the farmer had already sold part of the land to another buyer, but not the part where the ruins lay. Henry decided to buy the site of Knossos. The farmer told him there were 2,500 olive trees upon the land. Henry had them counted. There were only 888!

'The man is a cheat and a liar! I will not deal with him,' Henry declared angrily. He still had the mind of a merchant, and could not bear to be cheated, so he broke off the bargaining.

This was the great mistake of Henry Schliemann's life. At Knossos there were clues pointing to connections with the other civilizations that Henry had dug up at Mycenae and Tiryns. If he had uncovered Knossos and found the beautiful rooms and the gay-coloured frescoes there he might have discovered the link that bound these civilizations together. That would have been the brightest gem in his crown of success as an archaeologist. It fell to Arthur Evans to make the discovery afterwards.

Although in his later years Henry Schliemann travelled in many lands, especially in Egypt which he loved, he did no more digging such as he had done at Troy, Mycenae and Tiryns. He had many arguments with learned men in Europe who disputed the value of the digging he had done and the treasures he had found.

He went again to Troy, but while he was there he fell ill. He suffered great pain and swelling in his ear and he returned home to Athens. There the sea-bathing that he enjoyed so much only increased his ear trouble. He decided to go to Germany for an operation.

On the anniversary of their wedding day he wrote a loving letter to Sophia: 'We have lived together in health and happiness for twenty-one years. When today I look back over this long time I can never glorify our marriage enough, for you have always been my beloved wife, and, at the same time, my comrade, a guide in difficulties and a faithful and friendly companion, and, moreover, an exceptional mother. By Zeus! I will marry you again in the next world.'

Was there a sense of foreboding in this letter that they might never meet again?

Henry was operated on in Germany but the operation was not a success. The ear became inflamed and swollen again. He wrote to Sophia: 'The right ear has taken cold on a journey because I forgot to protect it with wadding. So I am deaf again and shall have to go back to the doctor tomorrow.'

He wrote also of his intention to return home to Athens for Christmas, a time when he always wanted to be with his wife and children. On this account he set out to join them when he was not fit to travel and should have been in bed.

He reached Naples on the journey home, but there the pain became so severe that he was not able to take the ship for Athens. He sent his family a telegram, 'Please delay Christmas celebrations'.

Next day he felt a little better, so he went with his doctor to see the ruins of Pompeii. The city had been buried under the lava when the volcano Vesuvius erupted and dug out many hundreds of years later. Still ancient ruined cities had the power to draw him as if by magic. The next day the raging pain in the ear was back again and on Christmas Day he collapsed in a street in Naples. He was carried to a police station where they found the name and address of his doctor on a paper in his pocket. The doctor was called and he had Henry carried back to his hotel. There, once more, the ear was operated on, but it was found that the inflammation had reached the brain. He became rapidly worse. The following day he passed away quietly while his doctors were trying to decide what they should do next. His body was taken to Greece. There, in Athens, he was laid to rest as he had wished, where he had found happiness among the Greeks whom he had loved and who loved him.

When William E. Gladstone, Britain's Prime Minister, heard of Henry Schliemann's death he wrote a letter in his own hand to Sophia: 'He had to encounter in the early stages of his work both frowns and indifference, yet the one and the other alike had to give way as the force and value of his discoveries became clear like mists upon the sun. The history of his boyhood and youth were not less remarkable than that of his later life. Indeed, they cannot be separated, for one aim and purpose moved them from first to last.'

It was true the young boy who was determined to find Troy and prove that Homer wrote true history and not fiction, had followed his 'one aim and purpose' faithfully all his life. In his last years he constantly wrote and spoke in the ancient Greek language. To a friend he said, 'Only Homer interests me. I am increasingly indifferent to everything else.'

For Henry Schliemann Homer was *truth*.

Among some archaeologists in Europe it was the fashion to run down Henry Schliemann as a mere seeker after treasure and gold. He was far more than that. He had the vision and force to excavate those old cities of Troy, Mycenae and Tiryns, and to show the world civilizations which existed over 3,000 years ago. He did not do it for the greed of gold, for he himself paid for the work of digging. The treasures he found were not kept for himself; he gave them to great museums in Athens and in Germany where we can see these priceless objects ourselves. Like Layard's, his work paved the way for many other archaeologists to continue where he left off.

William Dorpfeld went on digging at Troy with the help of Schliemann's money that Sophia gave to him after Henry's death. There he made many interesting discoveries of other cities below the one Schliemann had found.

Arthur Evans excavated the palace of Knossos in Crete and found many links between Crete and the people who lived at Mycenae and Tiryns. He also found quantities of inscribed clay tablets, proving that these ancient people could indeed read and write and possessed knowledge of mathematics and astronomy. If Evans, as a lad, had not listened to Henry Schliemann's lecture in London, he might never have been fired to follow in Schliemann's footsteps.

Henry Schliemann was the forerunner of all the men who excavated the ancient cities of the eastern Mediterranean. If we think of the young boy who slept under the grocer's counter and who, by the time he was twenty, taught himself to speak and write seven languages fluently, we realize what a long way Henry Schliemann travelled by his own efforts to become a great pioneer of archaeology.

Both Layard and Schliemann have been blamed by later archaeologists for sometimes destroying, in their digging, evidence of the former civilizations which inhabited the old palaces and cities.

No doubt if the mounds of Nimrud, Kuyunjik, Troy and Mycenae could have been excavated in modern times by new skills of archaeology, much more knowledge might have been gained. But would the mounds have been left undisturbed once men found they contained treasures of the past and that these treasures were valuable? In Egypt tomb-robbers seized and melted down many articles of gold and silver and sold others. The same might have happened at Troy and Mycenae if Henry Schliemann had not found the tombs first. He saw to it that the treasures went to museums.

In the same way Layard's discovery of the wonderful

carved wall sculptures and the magnificent library of clay
tablets in cuneiform writing in Sennacherib's palace enriched
the British Museum. He made sure that these priceless things
were preserved for all time for people to see. In their day
and age both Layard and Schliemann did their best with the
tools and skills they had to their hands. If they had not dug
when they did, the treasures might not have been there when
later archaeologists appeared on the scene.

Henry Layard's Turkish assistant, Hormudz Rassam, was
employed by the British Museum to work again on the
mound at Nineveh. In 1852 he found yet another chamber
stacked with clay tablets in cuneiform writing. This was the
royal library of King Ashurbanipal. Among these tablets he
also found the wonderful story-poem of Gilgamesh, a
Sumerian hero king, This epic also contained an account of
the Flood.

Other excavators followed. To Babylon in 1899 went a
German excavator, Robert Koldewey. He found the same
confused heaps of mud-brick walls that Layard had described.
For fifteen years he laboured there and found the great
city of King Nebuchadnezzar (605–562 B.C.) encircled by its
wall wide enough for a team of four horses to gallop
abreast of each other. He also found the remains of the great
Tower of Babylon itself and the terraces of its 'hanging
gardens'.

In 1887 an American team began to dig at Nippur.
Unfortunately they fell foul of the Arabs, and their tents were
fired and looted. The Americans returned in 1891, however,
and in three years' digging found 30,000 inscribed clay
tablets, many of them legal records and merchants' accounts,
and also some of the old Sumerian stories and legends.

In 1921, Sir Leonard Woolley, a noted archaeologist, went
to dig in southern Mesopotamia. He discovered the once
magnificent city of Ur, occupied for more than 4,000 years.

He, too, found wonderful royal tombs, rich in treasures of gold and silver.

To this day the work of digging out the old cities of Mesopotamia continues. Layard, indeed, had pioneered the way. To both Layard and Schliemann archaeology owes a great debt.

Remember especially that they dug *not* for treasure to enrich themselves but, as true archaeologists, to enrich the world with *knowledge*.